HEBREW CHRISTIANITY:
ITS THEOLOGY, HISTORY, AND PHILOSOPHY

HEBREW CHRISTIANITY: ITS THEOLOGY, HISTORY, AND PHILOSOPHY

Arnold G. Fruchtenbaum

BAKER BOOK HOUSE
Grand Rapids, Michigan

ISBN: 0-8010-3497-3

Copyright © 1974 by
Baker Book House Company
Grand Rapids, Michigan

Third printing, April 1978

All Scripture references are from
the American Standard Version, 1901

PHOTOLITHOPRINTED BY CUSHING - MALLOY, INC.
ANN ARBOR, MICHIGAN, UNITED STATES OF AMERICA
1978

This volume is dedicated to Mary Ann,
my wife and helpmeet,
with whom I am still in love.

PREFACE

There is an old axiom that states: Where there are two Jews, there are three opinions. Its truth is borne out in practice, for while there are Jewish leaders, no one can be called *the* spokesman for the Jews.

The same is true of Hebrew Christians (perhaps one of the strongest proofs that they are still Jews). I have spoken many times along the themes found in this volume, and I have always had one Hebrew Christian disagree with me on this point and another on that point, though always consenting that my basic theme was correct as far as they were concerned. So I suspect that every Hebrew Christian will disagree with some point in this book while consenting to the rest. Hence, I do not claim to be *the* spokesman for Hebrew Christianity, nor is this book the final word on the matter. Nevertheless, I do believe I have set down in these pages what Hebrew Christianity is today both in its theology and in the questions it is wrestling with. I am essentially stating the major themes of Hebrew Christianity today.

Special acknowledgments are made to my wife, who faithfully and patiently read the manuscript and made suggestions as to style; to Barb Taylor, who typed the manuscript; and to Mrs. Warren Graham (Linda), who checked the manuscript for grammar.

If there has been a failure to give credit where credit is due in any instance, then apology is offered and forbearance is requested. Most of the chapters in this book were written while I was overseas and living in Israel. Being away from my library, I did not have access to all of my source material.

ARNOLD G. FRUCHTENBAUM
Jerusalem, Israel

TABLE OF CONTENTS

CHAPTER I

JEWISHNESS AND HEBREW CHRISTIANITY: A MATTER OF DEFINITIONS

The title of this chapter may not reveal very much to many people. In fact, it may be confusing. If there is confusion, it is in all probability due to the definitions. This chapter is therefore devoted to defining the terms which will be used throughout the book.

One source of possible confusion is the term *Jewishness*. What really constitutes Jewishness? Who is a Jew? Does the term denote a religion, a race, an ethnic group, or a nationality?

In contrast to *Jew* is the term *Gentile*. Who is a Gentile? This too needs a clear-cut definition.

Another confusing term is *Christianity*. Is a Christian one who is born of Christian parents? Can one become a Christian merely by joining a church or by being baptized?

Then there is the term *Hebrew Christianity*. Who is a Hebrew Christian, or (as such a person is sometimes called) a Christian Jew? How is it possible for a person to be both a Jew and a Christian? Can the terms *Hebrew* and *Christian* be reconciled, or should those identifying themselves by both terms be classified as schizophrenics?

Jewishness: Who is a Jew?

We come then to the issue of who is a Jew. There are few topics in the Jewish world which have been more debated than this one. To this day there is no consistent definition. An inves-

1

tigation of several meanings is in order here before going on
to the preferred definition.

A Religious Definition

Several years ago, I left the United States for a year of study
in Israel. On the flight to Israel, I sat next to an Orthodox Jew,
a professor at Yeshiva University in New York City. When he
learned that I was a Hebrew Christian, he told me outright that
he considered me no longer a Jew. When I asked him for his
definition of a Jew, he replied that being a Jew (Jewishness) is
purely a religious matter. I asked him whether he considered
a Reform Jew to be Jewish. He answered that he did, because
a Reform Jew still practices Judaism in a limited way. Then I
asked him if he would consider an atheistic Jew or a communist
Jew to be Jewish. He said he would. I finally asked him how
he could consider a Jew who is an atheist or a communist,
having nothing in common theologically with Judaism, to be
a Jew, and then deny that I, a Hebrew Christian, am a Jew,
especially since I have much more in common theologically with
both Orthodox and Reform Jews. He had no answer, but still
maintained that the atheistic Jew is a Jew, whereas the Christian Jew is not.

If Jewishness is defined in terms of religion, then obviously
Hebrew Christians are not Jewish. But according to this definition neither are most Jews, because most Jews do not practice
Judaism. Defining Jewishness on a purely religious basis does
not satisfactorily explain who is a Jew.

A Nationalistic Definition.

I was studying at the Hebrew University in conjunction with
the American Institute of Holy Land Studies in Israel. One day
all the foreign students, numbering about 300, were called together for a special meeting. We were to be addressed by David
Ben Gurion, the George Washington of the state of Israel. In

his address he defined a true Jew as one who comes to Israel, settles in Israel, and raises his children in Israel. Jewishness then, in Mr. Ben Gurion's opinion, is defined in terms of Israeli nationalism, a nationalism based on Zionism. He did not recognize the Jewish people living outside of Israel as true or complete Jews. In fact, he considered them "Christianized Jews."

In the question and answer session that followed Mr. Ben Gurion's address, many American Jewish students, both Orthodox and Reform, challenged the speaker. The Orthodox students denied that Israel contained true Jewishness; one said that Israel is a state of Jews but not a Jewish state, because its law is not based on Orthodox Jewish Law. Though these Orthodox students contended that Jewishness was a matter of religion, Ben Gurion insisted that it was based on Israeli nationality. To him the Jews outside the land are in the *Galuth* (Exile). On the other hand, the Jews from outside the land did not consider themselves in the Exile but in the Dispersion. This meeting simply provided me with additional definitions of Jewishness.

The Benjamin Shalit Case

To this day in Israel the question of who is a Jew remains unclear. Twenty years after the state of Israel was reborn, the issue came up in the Israeli Supreme Court.

Commander Benjamin Shalit of the Israeli Navy and his Gentile wife are both atheists. When Commander Shalit sought to register his children as Jews by nationality but non-believers in religion, his request was refused by the Israeli Minister of the Interior. Commander Shalit took the matter to court, and since the case involved the definition of a Jew, nine of the ten chief justices presided over the hearing. The only reason all ten did not preside was to avoid a tie vote. (This number becomes more significant when it is realized that only three justices presided over the Adolf Eichmann trial.)

Shalit's argument was that the Israeli Minister of the Interior had no right to use religious standards in judging the secular issue of nationality. He maintained that as a non-believer he could not be forced to accept any decision grounded on religious law. He insists:

> It is not faith that unites us as a nation. Too many people do not practice religion for that. The cultural and sociological factors are the ones that determine who is a Jew. Not the memory of a primitive religion. My children were born in Israel, speak Hebrew, live in a Hebrew culture, and go to Hebrew schools. They know nothing else. How can the Interior Minister say that they are not Jews? (*Time,* November 29, 1968)

Shalit defines his Jewishness on the basis of identification:

> Religious observance is not part of the concept of Jewishness and the principal test of Jewishness is deliberate and declared association and identification with the Jewish people, its history, language, culture, and inheritance. He sought to persuade the court that anyone who declares himself to be a Jew by nationality is a Jew, even if he be an atheist, with the reservation however that he should not be so registered if he declares that he belongs to some other religious denomination. Jewishness to him then is not a biological question but one of historical, sentimental and intellectual identification. (*Jerusalem Post,* November 25, 1968)

Shalit contradicts himself in one major respect; on the one hand he says that a Jew is anyone who identifies himself culturally and sociologically with the Jewish people, while on the other hand he says that a Jew is no longer a Jew if he belongs to a religious denomination other than Judaism. This is a prejudicial statement against Hebrew Christianity. A Hebrew Christian can identify himself with the Jewish people just as much as Shalit can and at the same time believe that Jesus is the Jewish Messiah. In what way can Shalit, an atheist, deny that a Hebrew Christian is Jewish without contradicting himself and destroying the argument for his own Jewishness? To include himself as a Jew, therefore, Shalit rejects any and all religious definitions of Jewishness. But to exclude the Hebrew Christian he must revert to a religious definition.

The popular feeling is so strong on the question of who is a Jew that the National Religious Party of Israel announced it would pull out of the government coalition if the Supreme Court ruled in favor of Shalit, which the Court in fact did. The resulting pressure from the minority religious party and threats of a pull-out from the government coalition caused the government to reverse the decision the very next day and return to an ambiguous religious definition. It was good enough to keep the NRP in the coalition but not good enough to make them happy, based as it was on political expediency rather than on true conviction. And so the struggle continues. Later, a Hebrew Christian commented to me ironically, "So for one day I was a Jew again."

A Public Opinion Poll

As a consequence of the interest aroused by the Shalit case, a public opinion poll was held on the question. Fifteen hundred Jewish families were canvassed with the following results:

12% declared that a Jew is a person whose father or mother is Jewish or who has a Jewish spouse.

23% claimed that a Jew is a person who considers himself a Jew.

19% held that a man born to a Jewish mother or who converts to Judaism is a Jew.

13% said a Jew is one who lives in Israel or who identifies with the Jewish state.

13% stated that a Jew is one who observes the Jewish religious practices.

11% answered that a Jew is one who is raised and educated as a Jew.

9% said they could not define it.

These results were recorded in the *Jerusalem Post* of November 25, 1968. Of the definitions listed, only one excludes the Hebrew Christian, but at the same time it also excludes a large number of other Jews who do not observe Jewish religious practices. The other five definitions would by no means rule out the Hebrew Christian.

More could be said and other examples could be given to show the confusion in the Jewish world over definitions. But these should suffice to show that there is no uniformity or objective standard for defining Jewishness; virtually all definitions are subjective.

The Hebrew Christian Definition

The Hebrew Christian definition has an objective standard; it goes back to the very source of Jewishness, the Scriptures. The further any definition departs from the Scriptures, the foggier it gets. The Hebrew Christian is forced to define Jewishness in the biblical sense of the term, for to him the Scriptures are the source of authority. Hence the Hebrew Christian definition can also be called the biblical definition. The biblical basis for defining Jewishness lies in the Abrahamic Covenant in Genesis:

> Now Jehovah said unto Abram, Get thee out of thy country, and from thy kindred, and from thy father's house, unto the land that I will show thee: and I will make of thee a great nation, and I will bless thee, and make thy name great; and be thou a blessing: and I will bless them that bless thee, and him that curseth thee will I curse: and in thee shall all the families of the earth be blessed. (Genesis 12:1-3)

It is further described in two other passages:

For all the land which thou seest, to thee will I give it, and to thy seed forever. And I will make thy seed as the dust of the earth; so that if a man can number the dust of the earth, then may thy seed also be numbered. (Genesis 13:15-16)

And, behold, the word of Jehovah came unto him, saying, This man shall not be thine heir; but he that shall come forth out of thine own bowels shall be thine heir. And he brought him forth abroad, and said, Look now toward heaven, and number the stars, if thou be able to number them; and he said unto him, So shall thy seed be. (Genesis 15:4-5)

Later, the Abrahamic Covenant is confirmed through Isaac:

And Jehovah appeared unto him, and said, Go not down into Egypt; dwell in the land which I shall tell thee of: sojourn in this land, and I will be with thee, and will bless thee; for unto thee, and unto thy seed, I will give all these lands, and I will establish the oath which I swore unto Abraham thy father; and I will multiply thy seed as the stars of heaven, and will give unto thy seed all these lands; and in thy seed shall all the nations of the earth be blessed; because that Abraham obeyed my voice, and kept my charge, my commandments, my statutes, and my laws. (Genesis 26:2-5)

And Jehovah appeared unto him the same night, and said, I am the God of Abraham thy father: fear not, for I am with thee, and will bless thee, and multiply thy seed for my servant Abraham's sake. (Genesis 26:24)

After Isaac, it is reconfirmed through Jacob:

And, behold, Jehovah stood above it, and said, I am Jehovah, the God of Abraham thy father, and the God of Isaac: the land whereon thou liest, to thee will I give it, and to thy seed; and thy seed shall be as the dust of the earth, and thou shalt spread abroad to the west, and to the east, and to the north, and to the south: and in thee and in thy seed shall all the families of the earth be blessed. (Genesis 28:13-15)

From the Abrahamic Covenant a simple definition of Jewishness can be deduced. It lies in the repeated statement that a nation will come through the line of Abraham, Isaac, and Jacob, and thus defines Jewishness in terms of nationality. But unlike the view of many Israelis, this nationality is not confined to the state of Israel alone, but it includes all the Jewish people no matter where they are. It is a nationality based on descent and not on Zionism.

Biblically speaking, the Jewish people are a nation. Today we are a scattered nation, but we are, nevertheless, a nation. We are a nation because we are descendants of Abraham, Isaac, and Jacob. The implication of this definition is that no matter what a Jew does he can never become a non-Jew; no matter what the individual Jew may believe or disbelieve he remains a Jew. A Negro who is a Christian, Moslem, or Buddhist remains a Negro. A Chinaman who becomes a Christian remains Chinese; a Chinaman who remains a Buddhist also remains Chinese. The same is true of the Jew, whether Orthodox, Reform, atheist, or communist. If a Jew chooses to believe that Jesus is his Messiah, he too remains a Jew. Nothing, absolutely nothing, can change the fact that he is a descendant of Abraham, Isaac, and Jacob.

At this point the problem comes up of children of mixed marriages. These children are usually designated half-Jewish and half-Gentile. The theology of Judaism teaches that Jewishness is determined by the mother; if the mother is Jewish, then the children are Jewish. But again, this is a departure from the biblical norm and is therefore rejected by Hebrew Christianity. In the Scriptures it is not the mother who determines Jewishness but the father; consequently the genealogies of both the Old and New Testaments list the names of the men and not of the women, except in cases where a mother was notable in Jewish history. Thus if the father is Jewish, the children are Jewish. King David was definitely Jewish, although his great grandmother Ruth and his great-great grandmother Rahab were both Gentiles.

Gentile: Who is a Gentile?

If the Scriptures are used as the objective standard, then the definition of a Gentile is equally simple. A Gentile is simply anyone who is not a descendant of Abraham, Isaac, and Jacob. In short, a Gentile is anyone who is not a Jew. The implication again is that no matter what a Gentile does he can never become a non-Gentile.

But this raises the question of Gentiles who have converted to Judaism. Can they properly be called Jews? On the basis of Scripture, the answer is no. The Jew is the nationality; the religion is Judaism. Acceptance of Judaism by a Gentile does not make him a Jew but a proselyte. We see the distinction between Jews and proselytes in four passages. The first is found in Matthew 23:15:

> Woe unto you, scribes and Pharisees, hypocrites! for ye compass sea and land to make one proselyte; and when he is become so, ye make him twofold more a son of hell than yourselves.

It should be noted that these evangelists for Judaism are not said to seek to make one a Jew, but to make one a proselyte.

A second passage is Acts 2:10, which is at the end of a list of place names showing the origins of the multitude who had come to Jerusalem for the Feast of Pentecost. The list ends with the phrase "both Jews and proselytes." Again, there is that same distinction.

Acts 6:5 provides us with a third example:

> And the saying pleased the whole multitude: and they chose Stephen, a man full of faith and of the Holy Spirit, and Philip, and Prochorus, and Nicanor, and Timon, and Parmenas, and Nicolaüs a *proselyte* of Antioch. (Italics added)

In this passage a distinction is made between Nicolaus and the rest. The others were all Jews who had accepted Christ, but Nicolaus was a proselyte, a Gentile convert to Judaism who had accepted Christ.

The final example is found in Acts 13:43:

> Now when the synagogue broke up, many of the Jews and of the devout proselytes followed Paul and Barnabas; who, speaking to them, urged them to continue in the grace of God.

Again the same distinction is clearly made. Gentile converts to Judaism are never given the title of Jews.

The chief Old Testament example of a Gentile convert to Judaism is Ruth. Many Gentiles have tried to claim Jewishness on the principle of conversion based on Ruth's story. But Ruth is consistently called a Moabitess both before and after her acceptance of the God of Israel. This can be seen in Ruth 1:22; 2:2, 6, 21; 4:5, 10.

The conclusion is that a Gentile cannot do anything to become a non-Gentile.

CHRISTIANITY: WHO IS A CHRISTIAN?

We next attempt to find out who is a Christian. Again the Hebrew Christian is forced to go to the Scriptures to determine the true definition. The New Testament divides the world into three groups of people: Jews, Gentiles, and Christians (I Corinthians 10:32). It plainly teaches that no one can ever be born a Christian; everyone is either born a Jew or born a Gentile. A Christian, however, is either a Jew or a Gentile who has made a personal decision to become a Christian. He is not one who merely holds church membership or is baptized. These may follow the personal decision, but they cannot be the cause of one's becoming a Christian.

A Christian is a Jew or a Gentile who has come to realize that man is born in a state of sin and for this reason is separated from God. Thus the penalty for sin must first be paid if he is to come to know God in a personal way. However, being a sinner, an individual Jew or an individual Gentile cannot by himself pay the price or penalty for sin. This was the purpose of the Messiah, whom many Jews and Gentiles know to be Jesus. At his death, Messiah became the substitute for sin and so paid the penalty for it. Both the Old and New Testaments teach that without the shedding of blood there is no remission of sin:

> For the life of the flesh is in the blood; and I have given it to you upon the altar to make atonement for your souls: for it is the blood that maketh atonement by reason of the life. (Leviticus 17:11)

> And according to the law, I may almost say, all things are cleansed with blood, and apart from shedding of blood there is no remission. (Hebrews 9:22)

The basic content of faith (that is, what one must believe) is found in I Corinthians 15:1-4:

> Now I make known unto you, brethren, the gospel which I preached unto you, which also ye received, wherein also ye stand, by which also ye are saved, if ye hold fast the word which I preached unto you, except ye believed in vain. For I delivered unto you first of all that which also I received: that Christ died for our sins according to the scriptures; and that he was buried; and that he hath been raised on the third day according to the scriptures.

The content of faith is the gospel, involving the substitutionary death, burial, and resurrection of Christ. That which determines whether or not a person is a Christian is his willingness to place his faith, or belief, in Jesus as the substitute for sin. What he must do is described in John 1:12:

> But as many as received him, to them gave he the right to become children of God, even to them that believe on his name.

A person who at some point in his life personally received Christ as the one who made atonement for his sin experiences what it is to become a Christian. Thus if anyone says that he was born a Christian, this is an obvious sign, according to the New Testament, that he is not a Christian. Becoming a Christian is an experience by which one comes to know God through Jesus Christ and by which the sin separating the individual from God is removed. Christians are made, not born.

In summary, the New Testament teaches that everyone is born either a Jew or a Gentile. Christians are Jews and Gentiles who believe in the Messiahship of Christ.

Hebrew Christianity:
Who is a Hebrew Christian?

We finally come to the point toward which we have been working: defining Hebrew Christianity. In the common view, the term *Hebrew Christian* is a contradiction. One can be either a Jew or a Christian; to be both at once is, in this view, an impossibility.

One Jewish writer stated that the term *Jewish Christian* challenges logic. Another writer limited the title to Jewish believers in Christ during the first century but not thereafter. This view was held by a number of my former professors at the American Institute of Holy Land Studies. They used the term *Jewish Christians* in relation to Jewish believers during the first century but did not recognize the term as valid for Jewish believers today. But they never explained what they considered to be the difference between the first century Jewish believers and those of the twentieth century.

What then is a Hebrew Christian? If a Jew is a descendant of Abraham, Isaac, and Jacob, which we believe to be the proper definition, and if a Christian is one who has personally, by his own decision, accepted Jesus of Nazareth as his Messiah, then a Hebrew Christian is a Jew who believes that Jesus Christ is his Messiah. By faith Hebrew Christians align themselves with other believers in Christ whether Jews or Gentiles, but nationally they identify themselves with the Jewish people.

A Hebrew Christian therefore must acknowledge that he is both a Jew and a Christian. If a Jew accepts baptism solely to lose his identity as a Jew, he is by no means to be considered a Hebrew Christian; he is a renegade, a traitor, and an apostate. A Hebrew Christian is proud of his Jewishness. He is also proud of his faith in the Messiahship of Jesus. The experience by which a Jew becomes a Christian is just as much a mystery as that by which a Gentile becomes a Christian. The experience can be described, but it cannot be explained. The center of this experience is the person of Jesus Christ, although the causes which brought it about may differ. Perhaps it was the testimony of another Hebrew Christian, the printed word, preaching, or the reading of the New Testament. The causes vary, but the results are always the same: Jesus Christ becomes the object of faith and trust.

The distinction between Hebrew Christians and Gentile Christians, and the basis for this distinction, will be the theme of the next chapter.

Conclusion

It is clear from the Scriptures that Hebrew Christians never lose their Jewishness. Jewishness and Hebrew Christianity are not contradictory terms; each complements and fulfills the other. As witnesses to the truth of this assertion, two writers will be quoted, one from the first century and the other from the twentieth century. Both clearly acknowledge themselves to be both Jews and Christians.

The first writer is the Apostle Paul, one of the greatest Hebrew Christians ever known. He has been falsely charged with changing Christianity into a Gentile religion. It was not through

Paul that separation of church and synagogue was brought about, but through Bar Cochba, as will be seen in chapter three. Of Jewishness and Hebrew Christianity, Paul says:

> I say then, Did God cast off his people? God forbid. For I also am an Israelite, of the seed of Abraham, of the tribe of Benjamin. (Romans 11:1)

> Are they Hebrews? so am I. Are they Israelites? so am I. Are they the seed of Abraham? so am I. (II Corinthians 11:22)

> ... I yet more: circumcised the eighth day, of the stock of Israel, of the tribe of Benjamin, a Hebrew of Hebrews; as touching the law, a Pharisee; as touching zeal, persecuting the church; as touching the righteousness which is in the law, found blameless. Howbeit what things were gain to me, these have I counted loss for Christ. Yea verily, and I count all things to be loss for the excellency of the knowledge of Christ Jesus my Lord: for whom I suffered the loss of all things, and do count them but refuse, that I may gain Christ. (Philippians 3:4-8)

The second writer to be quoted is Marvin Lutzker, a twentieth century Hebrew Christian. He wrote an article for *The Los Angeles Times* in answer to a controversy between a Rabbi and a minister. The Rabbi Abraham J. Heschel had stated in a previous letter in the same newspaper that there can be no such thing as Jewish and Christian dialogue if the purpose of the dialogue is conversion. A local evangelical minister, Joseph A. Ryan, wrote in answer to Rabbi Heschel's article that in any Jewish and Christian dialogue, conversion of the Jew *must* be the purpose!

We quote from Mr. Lutzker's article as follows:

> I read with interest the statement by Dr. Abraham Joshua Heschel and the comment upon it by the Rev. Joseph A. Ryan, an evangelical minister. They both dwell on "conversion" of our Jewish people to Christianity. I, as a Jew, refute Dr. Heschel's statement that "interfaith dialogue can be meaningful

only if the intent is not conversion." I, as a Christian, refute Mr. Ryan's statement that the intent must be conversion. Statements referring to the "conversion" of the Jew to Christianity disturb me. I was born a Jew and will die a Jew. What does conversion imply? To me it implies the leaving behind of Jewishness and the acceptance of something quite foreign to Jewish thought, custom and belief.

Let us look at what acceptance of the Messiah's death on my behalf has done to and for my Jewishness. As a Christian, what part of my Jewishness have I given up? The one true God, the God of Abraham, Isaac and Jacob? Certainly not. Have I given up any part of the Old Testament? No. So then what have I been "converted" from and to what have I been "converted?" I imagine that our Jewish friends would answer that I no longer follow Jewish customs. This is true. However, Jewish customs of today are quite different than those of traditional Judaism. Reformed Judaism, too, has given up the traditional belief of the coming of the Messiah and other things. Have these Jews who attend a Reformed Temple been "converted" because they go into a temple without skull cap or prayer shawl? No, I have not been converted from anything. I am more of a Jew now than ever before, because I now read my Old Testament with understanding and belief.

What then is a Christian? A Christian is not such because he was born one, as many of our Jewish brethren think. Rather a Christian is one, Jew or Gentile, who has accepted the death of the Messiah on his behalf, thus fulfilling the Law of Moses, not ignoring it. The first Christian church was entirely composed of Jews. The first church was at Jerusalem; all of its many thousands of members were Jewish people who accepted His death as fulfillment of Isaiah's prophecy.

What does a Gentile who comes to Christ have to do? He has to accept the God of Abraham, Isaac and Jacob. He has to accept the Old Testament. In short, he has to accept basic Judaism, and in addition and most important, he has to accept the Jewish Messiah as his "corban," that is, his substitutionary sacrifice. This is basic Judaism: belief in our Torah; belief in our prophets' words; belief in our Old Testament.

Yes, I am a Hebrew Christian. I have not been "converted," but rather I have been completed in the acceptance of what was promised our Jewish people and the world.

Since the word "conversion" is used in Mr. Lutzker's article, it needs clarification. There is nothing wrong in the use of this word if it is used in the biblical sense; and in the biblical sense "conversion" is an experience resulting from an act that only God can accomplish. It involves turning from sin to God. No one can be "converted" by his own efforts or by the efforts of others.

Unfortunately, the word "conversion" has taken on a new connotation today. It has come to mean the act of switching religions or denominations. Biblically speaking, this is proselytism. A Jew who joins a church for the purpose of losing his identity is not a convert but a proselyte. To become a proselyte one has only to perform a human act, whereas to be converted one requires an experience which only God can perform. Thus when Mr. Lutzker in his article argues against "conversion," it must be made clear to the reader that he argues against the term as it is used in its modern sense and not as it is used in the Scriptures.

In conclusion, therefore, the words of these two Hebrew Christians, the Apostle Paul of the first century and Marvin Lutzker of the twentieth century, very well describe their beliefs and are in complete agreement with the Jewishness of Hebrew Christianity.

CHAPTER II

THE BIBLICAL BASIS FOR THE HEBREW CHRISTIAN DISTINCTIVE

Christians can become highly emotional when something they have held as truth is challenged. Often this is good, especially when it is a doctrine vital to faith that is in question. At other times such emotional responses can blind one to what the Bible may really say in contrast to what is held to be true. One particular area involves the idea of a Hebrew Christian distinctive in the Body of Christ. Many times when the idea that the Bible distinguishes between Jewish and Gentile Christians is postulated, verses are quickly quoted to the contrary, often out of context. "Galatianism" is the accusation often thrown against the one making the distinction, although few who make the charge really know the exact nature of the Galatian heresy.

I well remember an incident which occurred in homiletics class during my school days. It was my turn to preach. The sermon I had prepared had nothing to do with Hebrew Christianity in any way, but in an illustration which I gave I used the term *Hebrew Christian* only once in passing. This was enough, however, for the professor to become aroused. When I finished, the professor challenged my use of the term *Hebrew Christian*. His attack began with "I wonder what Arnold would say to . . ." and then he quoted a favored text about there being no difference between Jews and Greeks. When he finished his discourse, he quickly continued with the class and gave me no opportunity to satisfy his wondering. Yet, as we shall see, the Bible does teach that there is a Hebrew Christian distinctive in the Body of Christ.

But emotionalism is not the only problem which prevents an understanding of this doctrine. Two false views, which only tend to confuse the issue, are circulating among many Christians. One false view is that Gentiles, when they become believers in Christ, become "spiritual Jews." The other is that when a Jew and a Gentile become believers in Christ, all distinctions between the two are erased. The Gentile loses his "Gentilism," to coin a word, and the Jew his Jewishness, for there is no difference between the two whatsoever. Before the basis of the Hebrew Christian distinctive can be fully understood, we first need to deal with these two false views.

The False Views

1. *Gentile Christians are Spiritual Jews*

The first false view is that Gentiles become "spiritual Jews" upon believing in Christ. Logically, if believing Jews are spiritual Jews and believing Gentiles are spiritual Jews, then in the Christian realm there are no distinctions, since all are "spiritual Jews." Yet the Bible presents no such picture.

The Meaning of Spirituality. Perhaps the greatest problem with the term *spiritual Jew* is its use of the word spiritual to indicate some kind of national or racial transformation of the Gentile to a Jew. However, the Bible never uses spiritual in this sense.

Dr. Charles Ryrie, in his book *Balancing the Christian Life,* points out that three things are involved in the biblical teaching on spirituality: regeneration, the Holy Spirit, and time.[1] This means that spirituality only involves the believer; it is produced by the Holy Spirit, who brings the believer into a mature relationship with God; and obviously this takes time. So, as Dr. Ryrie states, "Spirituality is a grownup relation to the Holy Spirit." [2] A spiritual person is a believer who is under the control

1. Charles Caldwell Ryrie, *Balancing the Christian Life* (Chicago: Moody Press, 1969) pp. 12-13.
2. Ibid.

of the Holy Spirit. It is nothing more than that. So if a Gentile is under the Spirit's control, he is a spiritual Gentile. Likewise, a Jew who is under the Spirit's control is a spiritual Jew. There is no crossing of national lines. A Gentile remains a Gentile and a Jew remains a Jew; their spirituality is based on their relationship to the Holy Spirit.

Biblical Passages. But some will argue that all this is mere semantics and will use certain Bible texts to show that in some way Gentiles become Jews, whether by a spiritual transformation or by some other mystical act. One of these is Galatians 3:6-9:

> Even as Abraham believed God, and it was reckoned unto him for righteousness. Know therefore that they that are of faith, the same are sons of Abraham. And the scripture, foreseeing that God would justify the Gentiles by faith, preached the Gospel beforehand unto Abraham, saying, In thee shall all the nations be blessed. So then they that are of faith are blessed with the faithful Abraham.

Thus if Gentile believers become the children of Abraham by faith, does that not make them "spiritual Jews"? Not at all. Even in the physical realm not all the children of Abraham are Jews. Arabs are as much the descendants of Abraham as Jews, but in no way can they be classified as Jews. What is true of the physical is also true of the spiritual realm; being children of Abraham by faith is not enough to make one a Jew.

What then is the meaning of this passage? To begin with, it should be noted that the context is concerned with the question of whether salvation is by works or by faith. The Hebrew term for *children* or *sons* often has the meaning of followers. The point is that Abraham was declared righteous on the basis of faith and not on that of works. The true followers of Abraham, then, are those who are considered righteous on the same basis as Abraham, who practiced faith rather than works to attain salvation. The Gentile Galatians were never said to become Jews, but rather children of Abraham. Being a child of Abraham is not enough to make one a Jew.

Another verse often used is Galatians 3:29:

> And if ye are Christ's, then are ye Abraham's seed, heirs according to promise.

Since Gentiles become part of the seed of Abraham, does this not in some way make them spiritual Jews? Again the answer is negative; there are members of the physical seed of Abraham who are not Jews. The same is true in the spiritual realm. The meaning of this verse can best be understood if compared with Ephesians 2:11-13 and 3:6:

> Wherefore remember, that once ye, the Gentiles in the flesh, who are called Uncircumcision by that which is called Circumcision, in the flesh, made by hands; that ye were at that time separate from Christ, alienated from the commonwealth of Israel, and strangers from the covenants of the promise, having no hope and without God in the world. But now in Christ Jesus ye that once were far off are made nigh in the blood of Christ.

> To wit, that the Gentiles are fellow-heirs, and fellow-members of the body, and fellow-partakers of the promise in Christ Jesus through the gospel.

These Ephesian passages clarify what is meant by the Galatian statement of becoming heirs to the promises. It does not mean that Gentile believers become Jews in a mystical way, but rather that they become partakers in the blessings of the Jewish covenants and receive this privilege by faith. This act does not make them spiritual Jews but spiritual Gentiles. Even by being partakers, they do not share in all the facets of the covenants but only in the blessings involved in them. Things such as inheritance of the Land and circumcision, among others, are not appropriated by believing Gentiles. These elements are exclusively for the Jew.

The third passage for this idea is Romans 2:28-29:

> For he is not a Jew who is one outwardly; neither is that
> circumcision which is outward in the flesh: but he is a Jew who
> is one inwardly; and circumcision is that of the heart, in the
> spirit not in the letter; whose praise is not of men, but of God.

Since a true Jew is someone who is so inwardly, does not a believing Gentile meet that standard and so inwardly at least become a Jew? But to say this of Romans 2:28-29 is to ignore the
entire structure of Romans. The basic outline of the first three
chapters is as follows:

Salutation	1:1-7
Introduction	1:8-15
Theme	1:16-17
The World Under Condemnation	1:18-3:30
Gentiles	1:18-2:16
Jews	2:17-3:20
Conclusion	3:21-30

The section in which 2:28-29 is found is strictly a Jewish context. The Gentiles are nowhere in view, for Paul has finished
with them in 2:16. This verse can be better understood if taken
as the words of a Hebrew Christian speaking to non-Christian
Jews. In doing so he is using a play upon words. "Judaism" has
the root meaning of "praise." What this Christian Jew is saying
to non-Christian Jews is that outward Judaism is not enough to
make one righteous before God; this requires a Judaism of God.
The verse can be paraphrased, "Whose Judaism is not of men,
but of God." The true Jews are Jews who are so both outwardly
and inwardly.

2. There is no Difference
Between Jews and Gentiles
The first extreme argues against all distinctions by saying that
all believers are Jews. The second extreme tries to make all be-

lieving Jews into non-Jews, usually by employing out of context one or more of three passages having a phrase to the effect that there is neither Jew nor Greek. But a careful study of the very same passages in their context will show that the distinction between Jews and Gentiles is erased only in certain areas and not in all. Furthermore, a study of the text in the light of related passages clearly indicates that in other areas the distinction is still very much in effect, even within the body of believers.

The Passages Used. The first of the three passages used is I Corinthians 12:12-13.

> For as the body is one, and hath many members, and all the members of the body, being many, are one body; so also is Christ. For in one Spirit were we all baptized into one body, whether Jews or Greeks, whether bond or free; and were all made to drink of one Spirit.

The clear teaching of this passage is that entrance into the Body is by Spirit baptism. This is the only way and it is true for all, Jew and Gentile. There is no difference. This is all that can be deduced from this passage and no more.

The second passage is Galatians 3:28:

> There can be neither Jew nor Greek, there can be neither bond nor free, there can be no male and female; for ye all are one man in Christ Jesus.

The context of this passage deals with the matter of justification by faith. This is the only way anyone can be justified, whether Jew or Gentile. So in justification there is no distinction between the two. That alone can be deduced from this passage and no more.

The third passage is Colossians 3:11:

> Where there cannot be Greek and Jew, circumcision and uncircumcision, barbarian, Scythian, bondman, freeman; but Christ is all, and in all.

Again the context is the key to understanding this passage. Verses 5-11 are concerned with putting off the old nature and putting on the new nature. This is the true and only way toward maturity and spirituality for any believer, Jew or Gentile. Again, no more than that can be deduced from this passage.

The conclusion we are drawing is obvious. In the areas of justification, membership in the Body, and growth toward maturity, the procedure is the same for Jew and Gentile without distinction. However, this does not mean that in every area the distinctions are forever erased between the two.

The Evidence for Distinctions. As stated earlier, the study of these very same passages in the light of related passages will show that instead of teaching against all distinctions, the reverse is true. When critics of the Hebrew Christian distinction refer to these three passages, often only the "Jew and Greek" statement is cited and the rest is ignored. My homiletics teacher used this technique. But these verses not only state that there is no difference between Jews and Greeks, but they further state that there is no difference between bond and free, male and female. Yet the custom is often to avoid quoting the latter portion for reasons which will become apparent as we proceed. Now let us consider what the Bible has to say about the two latter groups and see if indeed the three passages teach that all distinctions are erased.

Bond and Free. There are five passages dealing with the bond and the free.

> Servants, be obedient unto them that according to the flesh are your masters, with fear and trembling, in singleness of your heart, as unto Christ; not in the way of eyeservice, as men-pleasers; but as servants of Christ, doing the will of God from the heart; with good will doing service, as unto the Lord, and not unto men: knowing that whatsoever good thing each one doeth, the same shall he receive again from the Lord, whether he be bond or free. And, ye masters, do the same things unto them, and forbear threatening: knowing that he who is both

their Master and yours is in heaven, and there is no respect of persons with him. (Ephesians 6:5-9)

Servants, obey in all things them that are your masters according to the flesh; not with eye-service, as men-pleasers, but in singleness of heart, fearing the Lord: whatsoever ye do, work heartily, as unto the Lord, and not unto men; knowing that from the Lord ye shall receive the recompense of the inheritance: yet serve the Lord Christ. For he that doeth wrong shall receive again for the wrong that he hath done: and there is no respect of persons. Masters, render unto your servants that which is just and equal; knowing that ye also have a Master in heaven. (Colossians 3:22-4:1)

Let as many as are servants under the yoke count their own masters worthy of all honor, that the name of God and the doctrine be not blasphemed. And they that have believing masters, let them not despise them, because they are brethren, but let them serve them the rather, because they that partake of the benefit are believing and beloved. These things teach and exhort. (I Timothy 6:1-2)

Exhort servants to be in subjection to their own masters, and to be well-pleasing to them in all things; not gainsaying; not purloining, but showing all good fidelity; that they may adorn the doctrine of God our Savior in all things. (Titus 2:9-10)

Servants, be in subjection to your masters with all fear; not only to the good and gentle, but also to the froward. (I Peter 2:18)

In all these passages, the Christian slave is to be in subjection to his master, even when the master is himself a Christian. The Christian master is never commanded to release his Christian slaves, which would be the practical outcome if all distinctions have indeed been erased. But the Christian freeman is still a freeman and the Christian slave is still a slave. How then are these passages consistent with the three verses cited earlier? Consistency is no problem. As far as membership in the Body, justification, and spirituality are concerned, the way is the same for the freeman and the slave. But once in the Body, these distinctions still exist.

Male and Female. Seven passages of Scripture clearly show that all distinctions between male and female certainly have not been erased. Subjection is the keynote to them all, as seen in position and function. I Corinthians 11:3-10 points out that the woman should keep her head covered in the assembly:

> But I would have you know, that the head of every man is Christ; and the head of the woman is the man; and the head of Christ is God. Every man praying or prophesying, having his head covered, dishonoreth his head. But every woman praying or prophesying with her head unveiled dishonoreth her head; for it is one and the same thing as if she were shaven. For if a woman is not veiled, let her also be shorn: but if it is a shame to a woman to be shorn or shaven, let her be veiled. For a man indeed ought not to have his head veiled, forasmuch as he is the image and glory of God: but the woman is the glory of the man. For the man is not of the woman; but the woman of the man: for neither was the man created for the woman; but the woman for the man: for this cause ought the woman to have a sign of authority on her head, because of the angels.

In I Corinthians 14:34-35, women are forbidden to speak in the church. This is to the extent that if she has any questions at all, she is to seek answers from her husband at home:

> Let the women keep silence in the churches: for it is not permitted unto them to speak; but let them be in subjection, as also saith the law. And if they would learn anything, let them ask their own husbands at home: for it is shameful for a woman to speak in the church.

Ephesians 5:22-25 points out the key idea of subjection:

> Wives, be in subjection unto your own husbands, as unto the Lord. For the husband is the head of the wife, as Christ also is the head of the church, being himself the saviour of the body. But as the church is subject to Christ, so let the wives also be to their husbands in everything. Husbands, love your wives, even as Christ also loved the church, and gave himself up for it.

In Colossians 3:18-19 we again have the idea of subjection. The husband is admonished to love his wife as the means of subjecting her.

> Wives, be in subjection to your husbands, as is fitting in the Lord. Husbands, love your wives, and be not bitter against them.

In I Timothy 2:11-12, women are forbidden to teach men, for in so doing they are exercising authority and overstepping their place of subjection:

> Let a woman learn in quietness with all subjection. But I permit not a woman to teach, nor to have dominion over a man, but to be in quietness.

In Titus 2:1, 3–5, the teaching of younger women to be in subjection to their own husbands is part of sound doctrine, and violation results in the word of God being blasphemed:

> But speak thou the things which befit the sound doctrine . . . that aged women likewise be reverent in demeanor, not slanderers nor enslaved to much wine, teachers of that which is good; that they may train the younger women to love their husbands, to love their children, to be sober-minded, chaste, workers at home, kind, being in subjection to their own husbands, that the word of God be not blasphemed.

I Peter 3:1 and 7 again point to subjection:

> In like manner, ye wives, be in subjection to your own husbands; that, even if any obey not the word, they may without the word be gained by the behavior of their wives.

> Ye husbands, in like manner, dwell with your wives according to knowledge, giving honor unto the woman, as unto the weaker vessel, as being also joint-heirs of the grace of life; to the end that your prayers be not hindered.

Now if all distinctions between male and female are erased, there would be no need for all these separate rules and injunctions. Do these passages then contradict the others which indicate no distinction between the male and female? Obviously not. Again, in the areas of membership in the Body of Christ, justification, and spiritual maturity, the formula is the same for both. There is not one way of salvation for the man and another for the woman. Spiritual maturity does not have separate systems, one for the male and another for the female. Both have entered the Body in the same way. But once in the Body, the man is still a man, and the woman is still a woman, and they differ in position and function.

Conclusion

To summarize, we have seen that the Bible does not support the idea of Gentiles becoming "spiritual Jews" when they believe. Rather, they are spiritual Gentiles when they are controlled by the Holy Spirit. Spiritual Jews are Jews who believe and who have a proper relationship to the Holy Spirit.

Furthermore, the Bible does not say that all distinctions between Jew and Gentile are erased when they believe. While it is very true that the way is the same for both, this does not mean that all other distinctions have been eradicated as well, anymore than all distinctions between bond and free and male and female have ceased to exist. The way of salvation, Body membership, and spiritual maturity is the same for both Jews and Gentiles. But in other areas distinctions remain.

THE HEBREW CHRISTIAN DISTINCTIVES

The question that now remains is, what are the Hebrew Christian distinctives in the Body of Christ? In what way, by position and function, does the Hebrew Christian differ from the Gentile Christian? The basis of the Hebrew Christian distinctive lies in four lines of biblical truth: the Abrahamic Covenant, the doctrine of the remnant, the doctrine of the olive tree, and the doctrine of the Israel of God.

The Abrahamic Covenant

(Genesis 12:1-3, 7; 13:14-17; 15:1-21; 17:1-21; 22:15-18; 26:2-5, 24; 28:12-15)

Galatians 3:15-18 draws a unique distinction between the Abrahamic Covenant and the Law of Moses:

> Brethren, I speak after the manner of men: Though it be but a man's covenant, yet when it hath been confirmed, no one maketh it void, or addeth thereto. Now to Abraham were the promises spoken, and to his seed. He saith not, And to seeds, as of many; but as of one, And to thy seed, which is Christ. Now this I say: A covenant confirmed beforehand by God, the law, which came four hundred and thirty years after, doth not disannul, so as to make the promise of none effect. For if the inheritance is of the law, it is no more of promise: but God hath granted it to Abraham by promise.

The point being made here is that the Law of Moses did not disannul the Abrahamic Covenant. The human illustration used is that of a human contract in antiquity. Once it was signed, it could not be changed. While additions could be made later, these additions could never nullify any point in the original. The Abrahamic Covenant was signed by God himself when he appeared in the form of fire and walked between the animals which Abraham had prepared (Genesis 15). While the Mosaic Law, coming 430 years later, added to it, the Law could in no way change it. Through the cross, however, the Mosaic Law (the addition) was rendered inoperative, but the Abrahamic Covenant (the original) is still very much in effect.

It is the continuity of the Abrahamic Covenant that provides the first basis of the Hebrew Christian distinctive. The covenant had four primary features to it. First of all, God promised to make a great nation of Abraham. This means the Jews as a whole. The Jews then are a nation because of their origin from Abraham, Isaac, and Jacob. Secondly, to this nation God has promised a land, once called Canaan, now called Palestine. It is totally irrelevant whether the Jews are in the Land or outside the Land or whether anyone else may control it by conquest or any other means, for the Land belongs to the Jews by divine right. Thirdly, those that bless this nation will be blessed and those that curse it will be cursed. This perhaps can be viewed as God's foreign policy to the Gentiles in their relationship to the Jewish people. Finally, the sign of the covenant for the members of this nation was circumcision, to be performed on the eighth day after birth.

Since the Abrahamic Covenant is still very much in effect, these four features also involve the Hebrew Christian both in his position and function. First of all, Hebrew Christians are still Jews, for they, like other Jews, are descendants of Abraham, Isaac, and Jacob. Secondly, the homeland for the Hebrew Christian is the land of Israel, and this is where his primary loyalty should be despite his place of residence. Hebrew Christians are in the *Diaspora,* but they are also in the *Galuth,* the Exile. Thirdly, the Gentile relationship to the Jews in the blessing and cursing aspects are as true for Hebrew Christians as for other Jews. Hebrew Christians who are blessed or cursed because of their Jewishness will find the blessers blessed and the cursers cursed. Finally, there is the matter of circumcision. Since Hebrew Christians still fall under the other provisions of the Abrahamic Covenant, they fall under this one as well. It is my conviction that Hebrew Christians should have their sons circumcised on the eighth day.

But does not the book of Galatians argue against the practice of circumcision? Yes and no. Circumcision for Gentiles, circumcision on the basis of the Mosaic Law, and circumcision for justification or sanctification are all wrong. Galatians condemns circumcision as a means for justification. Except for health and medical reasons, there is never any need or requirement for Gentile circumcision. Furthermore, Hebrew Christians who circumcise on the basis of the Law of Moses are also wrong, since the Law ended with Christ. But this same book clearly states that the Abrahamic Covenant is still very much in effect with all its features, and this includes circumcision. So circumcision on the basis of the Abrahamic Covenant is right and proper, and it is my conviction that it is still very much in effect for Hebrew Christians. Paul, who taught the Gentiles not to circumcise, did not do so with Jews; this is clear from Acts 21:17-26, and from Acts 16:1-3 when he had Timothy circumcised. It was not circumcision *per se* that was ruled out, but rather circumcision on the basis of the Mosaic Law.

The Doctrine of the Remnant

The second basis of the Hebrew Christian distinctive is described in Romans 11:1-7:

> I say then, Did God cast off his people? God forbid. For I also am an Israelite, of the seed of Abraham, of the tribe of Benjamin. God did not cast off his people which he foreknew. Or know ye not what the scripture saith of Elijah? how he pleadeth with God against Israel: Lord, they have killed thy prophets, they have digged down thine altars; and I am left alone, and they seek my life. But what saith the answer of God unto him? I have left for myself seven thousand men, who have not bowed the knee to Baal. Even so then at this present time also there is a remnant according to the election of grace. But if it is by grace, it is no more of works: otherwise grace is no more grace. What then? That which Israel seeketh for, that he obtained not; but the election obtained it, and the rest were hardened.

The question here is whether or not God has cast off his people Israel. Paul answers in the negative. His proof is himself; he is a Jew who believes. The critic may argue that the Jews who believe are a very small minority; so does it not follow that the nation has indeed been cast off? Again the answer is negative. What is happening now, Paul explains, is what has always happened throughout Jewish history, that is, only a remnant believes. It is always the remnant that believes. This was true in Elijah's day and it is true today. The fact that the majority do not believe is not evidence enough that the whole nation has been cut off. The point is that in Israel, past, present, and future, it is the remnant that is faithful to the revelation of God. This is also true in this present Dispensation of Grace; the Hebrew Christians are the remnant of Israel today. The remnant is always in the nation, not outside of it; the Hebrew Christians, the present-day remnant, are part of Israel and the Jewish people. Their Jewishness is distinct.

Isaiah 1:9 and 65:8 point out that it is the remnant that is keeping Israel as a whole alive:

> Except Jehovah of hosts had left unto us a very small remnant, we should have been as Sodom, we should have been like unto Gomorrah.

> Thus saith Jehovah, As the new wine is found in the cluster, and one saith, Destroy it not, for a blessing is in it: so will I do for my servants' sakes, that I may not destroy them all.

Because of the Hebrew Christian remnant, God did not permit the success of the many attempts throughout this age to wipe out the Jewish people. Again we see position and function in this basis of the Hebrew Christian distinctive.

The Doctrine of the Olive Tree

The third basis of the Hebrew Christian distinctive is in Romans 11:16-21 and 24:

> And if the firstfruit is holy, so is the lump: and if the root is holy, so are the branches. But if some of the branches were broken off, and thou, being a wild olive, wast grafted in among them, and didst become partaker with them of the root of the

fatness of the olive tree; glory not over the branches: but if thou gloriest, it is not thou that bearest the root, but the root thee. Thou wilt say then, Branches were broken off, that I might be grafted in. Well; by their unbelief they were broken off, and thou standest by thy faith. Be not high-minded, but fear: for if God spared not the natural branches, neither will he spare thee.

For if thou wast cut out of that which is by nature a wild olive tree, and wast grafted contrary to nature into a good olive tree; how much more shall these, which are the natural branches, be grafted into their own olive tree?

In this tree there are two types of branches, representing Jewish Christians and Gentile Christians. The Hebrew Christians are the natural branches; that is, we correspond to the very nature of the tree. It is as if the tree and the natural branches have the same blood type. The wild olive branches are the Gentile Christians. It is clearly stated that the presence of these branches in the tree is "contrary to nature." The blood type is different. There is an obvious composite difference between the two which makes them distinct from each other.

The Doctrine of the Israel of God

The fourth basis of the Hebrew Christian distinctive is seen in the narrow use of the term *Israel*. It should be pointed out that the term Israel is never used of Gentiles, whether they are believers or not, nor is it used of the church. It is used only of Jews. There are two passages dealing with this; the first is Romans 9:6-8:

But it is not as though the word of God hath come to nought. For they are not all Israel, that are of Israel: neither, because they are Abraham's seed, are they all children: but, in Isaac shall thy seed be called. That is, it is not the children of the flesh that are children of God; but the children of the promise are reckoned for a seed.

For a proper understanding of this passage, it is important to keep it in its strictly Jewish context. The point being made is

that there are two Israels: Israel the whole, composed of all
Jews; and Israel the elect, composed of all believing Jews, which
is the true Israel of God. Both groups are Jews and both groups
are called Israel, the difference being that the Jews who are of
Abraham by faith as well as by flesh are the true Israel. Israel
the whole, the Israel of the flesh, failed; but the elect of Israel,
the Israel of God, have not failed. Hebrew Christians, then, are
part of Israel the whole, but in particular they are the Israel of
God. Gentile Christians are not in this group. It is a position
which is distinct with Hebrew Christians.

The second passage is Galatians 6:16:

> And as many as shall walk by this rule, peace be upon them,
> and mercy, and upon the Israel of God.

As stated earlier, Galatians is concerned with Gentiles who were
attempting to attain salvation through the Law. The ones de-
ceiving them were the Judaizers, who were Jews demanding
adherence to the Law of Moses. To them, a Gentile first had to
convert to Judaism before he was qualified for salvation through
Christ. In verse fifteen Paul states that the important thing for
salvation is faith, resulting in the new man. He then pronounces
a blessing on two groups who would follow this rule of salvation by faith alone. The first group is the *them,* the Gentile
Christians to and of whom he had devoted most of the epistle.
The second group is the *Israel of God.* These are Hebrew
Christians who, in contrast with the Judaizers, followed the rule
of salvation by faith alone. Again a distinction between the two
groups is seen, for the Hebrew Christians alone are of the
Israel of God. It is a matter of position which here acts out a
definite function.

Conclusion

It is clear then that the Hebrew Christian is a distinctive element in the Body of Christ, and this distinctiveness is based on
four lines provided in the Scriptures. This distinctive feature in-

volves position (Jewish nationality, membership in Israel the whole, the Israel of God [the remnant], the natural branch in the olive tree) and function (circumcision, loyalty to Israel, the remnant that is keeping Israel alive, Gentile relationship in blessing and cursing). Although distinct from the Gentile Christians, the Hebrew Christians are nevertheless united with them in the Body of Christ. But does not this distinctiveness violate the unity? Not at all. For unity does not mean uniformity. God is a unity, yet the three persons (Father, Son, Holy Spirit) are distinct in position and in function (each member performs different roles in dealing with creation). All are equal, yet distinct. Distinctiveness in the Godhead does not violate unity, it only violates uniformity.

Looking at the Body of Christ from a different angle, we see that all believers are united in one body, but they are not all uniform. There are differences in position and function. All have spiritual gifts, but not the same number or kind. All are in equal standing before God, yet each is distinct. The same is true for the Jewish and Gentile element in the Body of Christ. In Christ, the two are one in unity but not in uniformity. Before God, we are all equal in terms of salvation but distinct in position and function.

A WARNING

I would like to close this chapter with a warning to my fellow Hebrew Christians. This warning is in the form of the biblical principle that to whom much is given, much is required (Luke 12:48). The fact that we are distinct from the Gentile Christian does not make us better. There is no room for pride or a feeling of superiority. God does not love us more than he loves them. This distinctiveness gives us a greater responsibility to God, to the Jews, to our fellow Hebrew Christians, and to the Gentile Christians as well, who are closer to us spiritually than unbelieving Jews. Much has been given to us out of pure grace. But so much more will be required of us.

CHAPTER III

THE HISTORY OF HEBREW
CHRISTIANITY

Having laid the foundations with the definitions of the terms used by Hebrew Christianity and shown the biblical basis for the Hebrew Christian distinctive, a short history of Hebrew Christianity is now in order before we proceed to the finer points of Hebrew Christian theology and philosophy.

A short history is what it will have to be since a full account would essentially require a volume of its own. Such a volume has been written by Hugh J. Schonfield, *The History of Jewish Christianity,*[1] but it is out of print at the time of this writing. Because of Schonfield's change of theological position from belief to unbelief, the book is unlikely to be republished, and one must explore used book stores in order to find it. But if the reader is interested in a more detailed historical account than is to be found in this chapter, the time it would take to search for the book would be well spent. Another volume containing a great deal of history is *The Jewish People and Jesus Christ*[2] by Dr. Jakob Jocz.

This history will be treated according to historical periods.

THE PERIOD OF A.D. 30-68

In this early period Christianity was Hebrew, and for all practical purposes it was a sect within Judaism. The Gentiles who

1. London: Duckworth, 1936.
2. London: S.P.C.K., 1954.

had become believers were already proselytes to Judaism and had embraced circumcision and submission to the Law of Moses. There does not appear to be any effort to reach Gentiles, and it was considered by many Hebrew Christians that Gentiles as Gentiles (non-proselytes) were unsavable.

A special revelation to the Apostle Peter was required to initiate Gentile Christianity. The conversion of Cornelius and his household, followed by the effective ministry of Paul among the Gentiles, created the first crisis in the church; what should be the status of Gentile Christians? The crisis itself, as well as the debates accompanying it, involved only the Hebrew Christians. The division was twofold: one camp stated that Gentiles are savable as Gentiles, and the other demanded that Gentiles first submit to circumcision and the Law of Moses (that is, become proselytes) before they could be saved.

The first crisis led to the Jerusalem Council, recorded in Acts 15, where the dissenting elements met to settle the matter. The testimonies of Peter and Paul held sway as they testified that Gentiles were experiencing the new birth simply as Gentiles. The result of this council is seen in the decree of James, the head of the Jerusalem church: the two groups were to be kept distinct but allied. The Apostles and the other Hebrew Christian leaders issued what might be called the Charter of Gentile Christianity, found in Acts 15:22-29:

> Then it seemed good to the apostles and the elders, with the whole church, to choose men out of their company, and send them to Antioch with Paul and Barnabas; namely, Judas called Barsabbas, and Silas, chief men among the brethren: and they wrote thus by them, The apostles and the elders, brethren, unto the brethren who are of the Gentiles in Antioch and Syria and Cilicia, greeting: Forasmuch as we have heard that certain who went out from us have troubled you with words, subverting your souls; to whom we gave no commandment; it seemed good unto us, having come to one accord, to choose out men and send them unto you with our beloved Barnabas

and Paul, men that have hazarded their lives for the name of our Lord Jesus Christ. We have sent therefore Judas and Silas, who themselves also shall tell you the same things by word of mouth. For it seemed good to the Holy Spirit, and to us, to lay upon you no greater burden than these necessary things: that ye abstain from things sacrificed to idols, and from blood, and from things strangled, and from fornication; from which if ye keep yourselves, it shall be well with you. Fare ye well.

That this edict of Gentile Christian conduct was different from the Hebrew Christian is evident from Acts 21:20-25:

And they, when they heard it, glorified God; and they said unto him, Thou seest, brother, how many thousands there are among the Jews of them that have believed; and they are all zealous for the law: and they have been informed concerning thee, that thou teachest all the Jews who are among the Gentiles to forsake Moses, telling them not to circumcise their children neither to walk after the customs. What is it therefore? they will certainly hear that thou art come. Do therefore this that we say to thee: We have four men that have a vow on them; these take, and purify thyself with them, and be at charges for them, that they may shave their heads: and all shall know that there is no truth in the things whereof they have been informed concerning thee; but that thou thyself also walkest orderly, keeping the law. But as touching the Gentiles that have believed, we wrote, giving judgment that they should keep themselves from things sacrificed to idols, and from blood, and from what is strangled, and from fornication.

So as far as personal salvation was concerned, Jews and Gentiles were on the same basis in their requirement of faith in Christ; yet the two conducted their lives quite differently.

But this is not the only place where the distinction was evident. It is also seen in the names by which the two groups were called, either by themselves or by others. The Gentile believers were called Christians (Acts 11:26), but the Jewish believers were called Nazarenes. This name comes out later in the accusation against Paul in Acts 24:5:

> For we have found this man a pestilent fellow, and a mover of insurrections among all the Jews throughout the world, and a ringleader of the sect of the *Nazarenes*. (Italics supplied)

This period saw the death of the first Christian martyr, Stephen (Acts 7:54-60), who was a Hebrew Christian; and it also witnessed the martyrdom of James, the first head of Hebrew Christianity, who was hurled from the Temple wall into the Kidron Valley below. This incident is recorded by Josephus.[3]

In summary, the first period witnessed the rise of Hebrew Christianity and its spread among the Jews. The Greek text states that "myriads" of Jews believed (Acts 21:20), which is quite a bit more than "thousands," as the word is translated in the English Bible. Following the crucifixion and resurrection of Jesus, the enmity of the Jewish religious leaders against Jesus was transferred to his followers. Several waves of persecution against the Hebrew Christians took place between A.D. 33 and A.D. 68; nevertheless, they lived among their own Jewish people, attended the Temple and synagogue services, and observed Jewish religious practices. The policy of Hebrew Christianity was a policy of distinction from Gentile Christianity, but there was still an alliance between them.

THE PERIOD OF A.D. 68-70

During this period the leader of Hebrew Christianity was Simon, son of Cleophas, a cousin of James and Jesus, who took over the leadership after the death of James. It was a difficult period for Hebrew Christianity. The revolt against Rome was on, and now after two years the Roman army had come and besieged Jerusalem. The Zealot Party inside the city was in control, and they rallied the people to fight. But the Hebrew Chris-

---

3. *Antiquities of the Jews* XX, ix, 1. It is also recorded by Eusebius in *Ecclesiastical History*, 2:23.

tians were caught in a dilemma. They remembered the following prophecy spoken by Jesus:

> But when ye see Jerusalem compassed with armies, then know that her desolation is at hand. Then let them that are in Judea flee unto the mountains; and let them that are in the midst of her depart out; and let not them that are in the country enter therein. For these are days of vengeance, that all things which are written may be fulfilled. Woe unto them that are with child and to them that give suck in those days! for there shall be great distress upon the land, and wrath unto this people. And they shall fall by the edge of the sword, and shall be led captive into all the nations: and Jerusalem shall be trodden down of the Gentiles, until the times of the Gentiles be fulfilled. (Luke 21:20-24)

According to this prophecy, the Temple and Jerusalem were both to be destroyed. The Hebrew Christians were told that when they saw armies surrounding Jerusalem, they were to flee. For this reason these Jewish believers refused to take up arms against the Romans, not because they wished to betray the Jewish cause, but because they felt bound to obey the words of Jesus of Nazareth. Now the sign that Christ gave, the surrounding of Jerusalem by armies, had arrived. So when for some unknown reason the Romans temporarily lifted the siege for a few days, the Hebrew Christians took the opportunity to flee to the city of Pella in the Transjordan. Soon after that, the Romans returned and besieged Jerusalem again, and in A.D. 70 Jerusalem and the Temple were both destroyed.

It is at this time that the term *Meshumod* or *Meshumodim* began to be applied by the Jewish community to Hebrew Christians, and it is still used today. It comes from a Hebrew word meaning to destroy, but it is used in the sense of traitor.

Meanwhile, the Hebrew Christians continued living in Pella, and a description of their style of life comes down to us in the writings of Ireneus:[4]

4. *Against Heresies* 1:26.

> They practice circumcision, persevere in the observance of
> those customs which are enjoined by the Law, and are so
> Judaic in their mode of life that they even adore Jerusalem as
> if it were the house of God.[5]

This statement from a leader of Gentile Christianity was derogatory; it was actually a complaint, but it nevertheless shows the faithfulness of the Hebrew Christians to Jewishness, although it was necessary for them to desert Jerusalem in obedience to the command of Jesus the Messiah.

The destruction of Jerusalem and the Temple was taken by the Hebrew Christians as the fulfillment of the words of Jesus and accepted by them as further evidence of his Messiahship. This led many Jews to accept Jesus as the Messiah.

THE PERIOD OF A.D. 70-132

The destruction of Jerusalem and the Temple and the resulting dispersion of the Jews from the Land brought about a national and religious crisis in the Jewish world. Two questions were raised that had to be answered: (1) how can Judaism, deprived of the Temple and the sacrificial system, survive religiously? and (2) how can the Jewish people, scattered in a hostile Gentile world, survive nationally? The solutions were developed over a period of years: (1) biblical Judaism was set aside and replaced by Rabbinical Judaism, the rabbi replacing the priest as the leader of Jewish life, and (2) the synagogue became the center of Jewish life.[6]

And so Rabbinical Judaism was born. This new form was unacceptable to Hebrew Christians because of their faith and conviction that Jesus the Messiah, by his substitutionary death and resurrection, fulfilled the Mosaic Law and brought in a new

5. As quoted by Hugh J. Schonfield in *The History of Jewish Christianity*, p. 54.

6. Jakob Jocz, *The Jewish People and Jesus Christ*, p. 40.

era of grace. The battles raged; but even during the controversies after the destruction of Jerusalem, the Hebrew Christians continued to live in the midst of other Jews.

Other incidents of this period included the campaign of Domitian to destroy the house of David. In these persecutions the two grandsons of Jude were arrested (the same Jude who authored the New Testament epistle, the brother of James and half brother of Christ). The grandsons were later released,[7] but under Emperor Trajan, Simon, son of Cleophas, the second head of Hebrew Christianity, was killed.[8]

The Hebrew Christian community returned to Jerusalem and again set up its assembly there. The names of the next thirteen leaders of Hebrew Christianity who followed James and Cleophas have come down to us:[9] Justus I, Zaccheus, Tobias, Benjamin, John, Matthias, Phillip, Seneca, Justus II, Levi, Ephraem, Joseph, and Judah.

In summarizing this period, the Hebrew Christians clearly emerged again as a distinct element within the Jewish community, although they were somewhat less trusted. The rift caused by the desertion of Jerusalem proved to be a temporary one, and a partial reconciliation did come about despite Hebrew Christian opposition to the new Judaism of the rabbis.

THE PERIOD OF A.D. 132-135

The events of these three to four years were to change the whole course of Hebrew Christianity for a long, long time to come, to the detriment of Hebrew Christian coexistence with the Jewish community. These were the years of the second Jewish revolt against Rome under Bar Cochba.

7. Eusebius, *Ecclesiastical History,* 3:20.
8. Ibid., 3:32.
9. Ibid., 4:5.

When the revolt first broke out, the Hebrew Christians joined the fighting with their Jewish brethren, identifying themselves nationally since this was a national cause. This time the limitation that kept the Hebrew Christians from the first revolt was no longer applicable; so they took up their swords and rallied under Bar Cochba's banner. As long as the banner was strictly political and national, the Hebrew Christians had no problem. If things had continued in this pattern throughout the whole course of the revolt, the history of Hebrew Christianity might have been radically different.

But as the revolt progressed, Rabbi Akiba made the sad blunder of declaring Bar Cochba the Jewish Messiah. From this point on, the revolt was led under the messianic banner of Bar Cochba, and the element of religion now entered in. This switch of policy forced the Hebrew Christians to pull out of the war since they refused to acknowledge Bar Cochba as the Jewish Messiah.

The result was tragic. It was at this stage of Hebrew Christian history that a complete break took place between the Jewish Christians and the rest of the Jewish people. If anyone can be blamed for turning Christianity into a "Gentile religion," it is Bar Cochba and not Paul, who has often been so accused. Jewish Christians were now to be ostracized. Non-Christian Jews were to have no dealings with Hebrew Christians; even if a Jew were dying, he was to refuse help from a Hebrew Christian doctor. To the *Shmoneh Esreh,* the Eighteen Benedictions, was added a nineteenth aimed directly at the Hebrew Christians:

> Let there be no hope for the apostates and let all the sectaries perish in a moment.

But the forced separation of Hebrew Christians from the Jewish community was not the only result of the Bar Cochba revolt. After the revolt collapsed, Jerusalem was plowed, rebuilt by the Romans, and renamed Aelia Capitolina; it became off-limits for all Jews, including the Hebrew Christians. Jerusalem thus became a Gentile city, and the Jerusalem church became a Gentile church and largely remains so to the present.

In closing this section, it must be stressed again that the Hebrew Christians did not leave the synagogue of their own volition. They were forced out by the leadership of that day.

The Period of a.d. 135-1800

The results of the Bar Cochba revolt set the stage for Hebrew Christianity for the next seventeen centuries. Its history during this long period is very sketchy for two reasons. First, there is the problem of distinguishing between those Jews who became believers in Jesus by conviction and those who were forced to convert. The latter can hardly be called Hebrew Christians; there is a world of difference between Jewish Christians and Christianized Jews. Second, there is the shift of Hebrew Christian policy from distinction to assimilation into the Gentile-cultured church. Often the next step after a Jew accepted Christ was to give up everything Jewish, even exchanging his Jewish name for a Gentile one. Nevertheless, in spite of these problems there has always been a traceable line of Jewish believers in the Messiahship of Christ. Sometimes the numbers have been small, but there has always been a number. These have always been active in spreading the gospel. After a detailed study, Schonfield concludes:

> Thus at home and abroad Jewish Christianity was active in spreading the glad tidings by every available channel, among rude savages and learned theologians, among Jews and Greeks, Barbarians, Scythians, bond and free.[10]

Even soon after the Bar Cochba revolt, Jews were turning to Christ despite the separation, and Hebrew Christianity was still something of a force in the Jewish communities of Palestine. This is evident from Jewish writings of the Talmudic Period.

10. Schonfield, *Jewish Christianity*, p. 74.

Five of these writings will be quoted,[11] and it should be noted how often Hebrew Christians are still referred to as Nazarenes.

> The case of Rabbi Eliezer who was arrested for heresy, and they brought him to the tribunal for judgment. The Roman governor said to him, Does an old man like you occupy himself with such matters? He replied, Faithful is the judge concerning me. The Governor supposed that he referred to himself, but he was really thinking of his Father in heaven. Said the governor to him, Since you place yourself confidently in my hands, so let it be. Perhaps these societies err concerning these things. *Dismissus!* Behold, you are released.
>
> When he had been freed from the tribunal, he was troubled because he had been arrested for heresy. His disciples came in to console him, but he would not take comfort. Rabbi Akiba entered, and said to him, Rabbi, perhaps I can explain the cause of your grief. He answered, Say on. He said to him, possibly one of the heretics spoke an heretical saying to you, and it pleased you. He said, By heaven, you have reminded me! Once I was walking along the upper street of Sephoris, and I met Jacob of the village of Sichnin, and he quoted an heretical saying to me in the name of Jesus and it pleased me. (T. Hullin ii, 24)

The fact that Rabbi Akiba plays a major role in this account is significant since it was his declaration of the messiahship of Bar Cochba that caused the Hebrew Christians to pull out of the war and hence be declared heretics. And so a mere repetition of or being pleased with a saying by Jesus could cause havoc in one's life, as it did in Rabbi Eliezer's.

> A man shall have no dealings with the heretics, nor be cured by them, even for the sake of an hour of life. There was the case of Ben Dama nephew of Rabbi Ishmael, whom a serpent bit. There came Jacob the heretic of the village of Sechanya to cure him (in the name of Jeshu ben Pandera); but Rabbi Ishmael would not allow him. Ben Dama said to him, Rabbi Ishmael, my brother, do allow him, that I may be cured and

11. As quoted by Hugh J. Schonfield in *The History of Jewish Christianity,* pp. 75-81.

> I will produce a text from the Law to prove that this is permitted. But hardly had he finished his discourse when his soul departed, and he died. (Aboda Zara 27b)

> The grandson of Rabbi Joshua ben Levi had something stuck in his throat. There came a man and whispered to him in the name of Jesus, and he recovered. When the healer came out, Rabbi Joshua said to him, What was it you whispered to him? He said to him, A certain word. He said to him, It had been better for him that he had died rather than that. (Shabbath 14b)

These quotations show just how extreme the prejudice against Hebrew Christians was, for Judaism allows the breaking of any and all law if the result is the saving of life. But in these cases death was preferred to being cured by a Hebrew Christian—a rather extreme position indeed.

In the first two quotations reference is made to Jacob of the village of Sichnin in the Galilee. All that is known of him is found in quotations like those above (obviously negative). But they do show that whoever he was, he was an able and effective Hebrew Christian witness, for the rabbis did all they could to keep other Jews away from him.

> The Nazarene Day: On the eve of the Sabbath they did not fast out of respect to the Sabbath; still less did they do so on the Sabbath itself. Why did they not fast on the day after the Sabbath? Rabbi Johanan says, Because of the Nazarenes. (B. Taanih, 27b)

The Sabbath is a time of eating; so Jews generally do not fast before or on the Sabbath. The question is, why not fast at any time on the day after the Sabbath? The answer is, to avoid showing any respect to the day regarded as special by the Nazarenes. The significance of this quotation seems to be that Hebrew Christians were worshipping on Sunday.

> Nazarenes are worse than Gentiles: Gentiles, and those that keep small cattle and those that breed the same are neither

helped out of a pit nor cast into it. The heretics and the
apostates and the informers are cast in and not helped out.
(Tos. Baba Mezia. ii, 33)

To put Hebrew Christians beneath the Gentiles was really placing them on a low status. What these quotations show is that
soon after the Bar Cochba revolt the Hebrew Christian element
was still there, but the campaign to ostracize them from the
Jewish community was strong. However, there were Hebrew
Christian communities all over Palestine and other parts of the
Middle East right up to the Arab conquest.

One of the most important Hebrew Christians from this
period was Hegesippus, who was perhaps the first church his-
torian. He was born in Palestine around A.D. 140 at the time
when Hebrew Christians were being ostracized from the Jewish
community. His history was written in a five-volume work
which has now been lost. The little that is known of it comes
from Eusebius, who quotes heavily from Hegesippus in his
Ecclesiastical History. Should these works ever be found, they
are sure to carry a wealth of information regarding this early
period of Hebrew Christianity. But for now we can only be
thankful for what we do have through the quotations by Eusebius.

During the time of Constantine, there were two Hebrew
Christians who made an impact in the church. One was Epi-
phanus, who became the Bishop of Constantinople. In his book
Panarion he tells of several Jews who became believers. The
other was Count Joseph, a rabbinical student in Tiberias. After
his conversion, he devoted himself to building churches in the
towns of Palestine; he did so in Tiberias, Nazareth, and Sephor-
ris, cities which were populated by Jews.

Nevertheless, while the above two maintained their Jewishness, others were unable to do so. The church, now becoming
a power in the Roman Empire, issued special professions of faith
for Jews wishing to convert. These required not only that they

renounce Rabbinical Judaism, but that they repudiate their very Jewishness as well, even to the point of adopting Gentile names.[12]

The Arab invasion of the sixth century brought Hebrew Christianity in Palestine to an end and moved its center to Europe.

During the Middle Ages, many Jews who turned to Christ followed the path of assimilation and were totally lost to the Jewish culture. There were some Jewish Christian attempts to evangelize the Jews, but these attempts were foiled by the church, which preferred using the sword to using the gospel.

One incident that comes down to us from this period is the Disputation in Aragon. Lasting over a year, from 1413-14, the debate was between two Hebrew Christians, Joshua ben Joseph Al Lorqui and Andreas Beltram, and twenty-two rabbis. The two Hebrew Christians handled themselves so well that it resulted in the conversion of five thousand Jews.[13]

When Columbus set sail for America, there were many Jews on his ship, and among them some Hebrew Christians. During the period of Spanish supremacy, a number of the wealthy and influential families were Hebrew Christians, such as the Carthagenas family of Spain and the Pierleonas family of Italy.

In England special homes, called 'converts' homes', were erected for Hebrew Christians and financed by the government. These became necessary for Jewish believers because at baptism they were deprived of all their possessions. These homes gave them the opportunity to get back on their feet. Also in England, the personal physician to Queen Elizabeth I, Dr. Rodrigo Lopez, was a Hebrew Christian.

During the Inquisition in Spain, it was not only the Christianized Jews (those converted by force) who suffered torture

12. Schonfield quotes ten such professions of faith on pages 107-12.
13. Schonfield, *Jewish Christianity,* pp. 150-51.

and death, but also the sincere Jewish Christians. The death penalty was meted out to Jewish Christians because they often continued to observe Jewish religious practices.

Often during this long period, Hebrew Christians stemmed outbreaks of anti-Semitism, saving many Jewish lives.

Regarding the Reformation, Schonfield writes:

> Thus behind the Reformation, as behind almost every spiritual and political movement of note, one finds the personality of a Jewish Christian.[14]

A long list can be drawn up of Jews who became believers in Christ and heavily contributed to the progress of the Reformation.

To summarize what is already a summary of this period, Jews continued coming to Christ and their policy was one of assimilation. The resulting sad fact was that no Hebrew Christian distinctive was maintained; there was no real development of a true Hebrew Christianity. Jewish Missions did not exist; there was no Hebrew Christian center to testify and bear witness to the Jewish wing of the Body of Christ.

The 19th and 20th Centuries

The nineteenth century saw a reversal from the policy of assimilation to that of a distinction, although the exact nature of the distinction has not always been very clear. The origin of the modern Hebrew Christian movement as we know it today coincides with the time of the national reawakening of the Jewish people about a hundred years ago. Jewish Missions now came into their own as Jews approached Jews with the gospel of Christ.

In 1865 the International Hebrew Christian Alliance was founded in London on the premise:

14. Ibid., p. 169.

Let us not sacrifice our identity. When we profess Christ, we do not cease to be Jews; Paul, after his conversion, did not cease to be a Jew; not only Saul was, but even Paul remained, a Hebrew of the Hebrews. We cannot and will not forget the land of our fathers, and it is our desire to cherish feelings of patriotism. . . . As Hebrews, as Christians, we feel tied together; and as Hebrew Christians, we desire to be allied more closely to one another.[15]

Later, in 1915, the Hebrew Christian Alliance of America was founded.

The nineteenth century saw at least a quarter of a million Jews come to Christ, and many of them made invaluable contributions in their respective fields. The list would include Benjamin Disraeli, Prime Minister of England who gained the Suez Canal and India for the British Empire; Alfred Edersheim, whose *Life and Times of Jesus the Messiah* is still the classic on the life of Christ; Felix Mendelssohn, the great composer; Johann August Wilhelm Neander, whose work in church history became the basis for all future works in this field. Franz Delitzsch, who along with Keil wrote the Old Testament commentary that is still the finest and the standard in this field (his translation of the New Testament into Hebrew is still the translation used in Israel today); Bishop Samuel Joseph Schereschewsky, the translator of the Chinese Bible; David Baron, whose commentaries on Isaiah 53 and the book of Zechariah have yet to be superseded; Bishop Michael Solomon Alexander, the first Anglican bishop of Jerusalem; Rabbi Leopold Cohn, founder of the American Board of Missions to the Jews, the largest Jewish mission in the world; Rabbi Joseph Rabinowitz, founder of the Hebrew Christian Synagogue in Hungary; Rabbi Isaac Lichtenstein, who also had a Hebrew Christian Congregation in Europe; and many others.

And so we come to modern Hebrew Christianity. Its separate and distinct existence is marked by a deep awareness of its kin-

15. Ibid., p. 222.

ship with the Jewish people and of the unique character of its mission to maintain in their midst a candlestick of witnesses to the Messiahship of Jesus.[16]

CONCLUSION

But not all the smoke has as yet been cleared. Hebrew Christianity is still striving to maintain a policy of distinction, but there is not full agreement as to how this should be done or the reasons for it. At times the fight against the extreme of assimilation was and is being countered by the other extreme of separation from Gentile Christianity. But I feel that separation is not the biblical pattern any more than assimilation is. The biblical pattern is a middle course, that is, the maintaining of the Hebrew Christian distinctive within the whole Body of Christ. The theology and the biblical basis for this distinctive has already been dealt with in chapter two. The methodology of maintaining this distinctive in a Gentile-cultured Christian majority is part of the concern of the following chapters.

POSTSCRIPT

As this is being written, great things are beginning to happen in the field of Jewish missions. Among Jewish young people there has been a tremendous turning to Christ, often in numbers which were inconceivable only a few short years ago. Hebrew Christian movements such as the San Francisco-based Jews for Jesus have had phenomenal success in confronting Jews with the claims of Christ. The new surge of Hebrew Christianity is making itself felt in other age groups as well.

But with this new surge have come growing pains. Some extreme elements are hotly advocating dropping terms such as

16. Arthur Kac, *The Spiritual Dilemma of the Jewish People* (Chicago: Moody Press, 1963), p. 122.

"Christ" or "Christian" on the flimsy ground that these terms are Greek rather than Hebrew. Others wish to claim that they are representing a Messianic movement "within Judaism," which in no way.can really be true. It is my prayer that those advocating such measures will see the need for balance.

It is gratifying, however, to see that the majority of the present wave of Jewish believers are rejecting such extremes. It is also gratifying to see them reject assimilation while maintaining the distinction in some unique and exciting ways. One example is the writings of Bob Friedman, which portray a distinctive Hebrew Christian humor. His book *What's a Nice Jewish Boy Like You Doing in the First Baptist Church* is a classic. In the past, what has been called Hebrew Christian music has really been Gentile music with Jewish words. Now, however, we are seeing an emergence of a truly Hebrew Christian musical motif. Stuart Dauerman's *Songs for the Messiah* and the Hebrew Christian singing group *The Liberated Wailing Wall* are indicative of the new trend.

A new sense of boldness in the Hebrew Christian movement is evident from the confrontation tactics of the Jews for Jesus and the mass media approach pioneered by the American Board of Missions to the Jews.

For the first time since the first century the rabbis are considering the Hebrew Christian movement a threat. The Messiahship of Jesus is becoming a live issue in the Jewish community.

A whole new chapter is now in the process of being written in the history of Hebrew Christianity.

CHAPTER IV

MESSIANISM

Do Hebrew Christians believe differently from Gentile Christians? Regarding the basic doctrines of the Christian faith, the answer is no. Among fundamental believers certain teachings are held in common, such as the substitutionary atonement of Christ for our sins. On some minor issues, such as baptism, there are differences of opinion. These differences, however, are not between the two types of Christians but between believers in general; Jewish and Gentile Christians will be found on each side.

While holding in common with Gentile believers the basic tenets of the Christian faith, Hebrew Christians, because of their background, will stress particular aspects with which Gentile Christians would generally agree but would not emphasize. So when we talk about a Hebrew Christian theology, we are in most (but not all) cases talking about points of emphasis. The purpose of the following chapters is not to develop a Hebrew Christian theology which differs from that of Gentile Christianity, but to bring out and develop the points of emphasis. One emphasis is in the area of Messianism.*

The Scriptures teach that there are three lines of Messianism. Generally only one of these lines is stressed by the Gentile Christian, but Hebrew Christianity would emphasize all three.

The Messianic Program

The first of these lines is a *Messianic Program*. The Old

---

*— e.g., the writings of Dr. Arthur W. Kac.

52

Testament is rich with prophecies concerning this program, and perhaps the most complete work in this area is Alva J. McClain's book *The Greatness of the Kingdom*.[1] For our purpose one example will suffice to show what the Messianic Program is all about.

> But in the latter days it shall come to pass, that the mountain of Jehovah's house shall be established on the top of the mountains, and it shall be exalted above the hills; and peoples shall flow unto it. And many nations shall go and say, Come ye, and let us go up to the mountain of Jehovah, and to the house of the God of Jacob; and he will teach us of his ways, and we will walk in his paths. For out of Zion shall go forth the law, and the word of Jehovah from Jerusalem; and he will judge between many peoples, and will decide concerning strong nations afar off: and they shall beat their swords into plowshares, and their spears into pruning-hooks; nation shall not lift up sword against nation, neither shall they learn war any more. But they shall sit every man under his vine and under his fig-tree; and none shall make them afraid: for the mouth of Jehovah of hosts hath spoken it. (Micah 4:1-4)

The basic outline of the Messianic Program is: (a) Jerusalem will become both the capitol of the world kingdom and its spiritual center; (b) from this spiritual center a spiritual movement will go into the nations of the world; (c) one result of this spiritual movement will be world peace, since differences between nations will be decided by decisions or decrees coming out of Jerusalem; and (d) a second result will be personal peace and prosperity.

The Messianic Person

The second of these three lines of Messianism is a *Messianic Person*. Again the Old Testament explains and describes this

1. Grand Rapids: Zondervan, 1959.

person. Isaiah states that he is to be a descendant of the house of David:

> And there shall come forth a shoot out of the stock of Jesse, and a branch out of his roots shall bear fruit. (11:1)

Chapter 53 of Isaiah describes the suffering and death of the Messianic Person. In this chapter he is called the "Servant of Jehovah," and the chapter outlines the program of his first coming. It states that:

a) The Servant of Jehovah is a suffering Servant:

> He was despised, and rejected of men; a man of sorrows, and acquainted with grief . . . (53:3)

b) The Servant of Jehovah is an innocent sufferer:

> . . . he had done no violence, neither was any deceit in his mouth. (53:9)

c) The Servant of Jehovah is a willing sufferer:

> He was oppressed, yet when he was afflicted he opened not his mouth; as a lamb that is led to the slaughter, and as a sheep that before its shearers is dumb, so he opened not his mouth. (53:7)

d) The Servant of Jehovah suffers for the sins of Israel:

> But he was wounded for our transgressions, he was bruised for our iniquities; the chastisement of our peace was upon him [i.e., the punishment was laid upon him for our well-being]. . . . (53:5)

e) The Servant of Jehovah dies for the sins of Israel:

> . . . he was cut off out of the land of the living for the transgression of my people to whom the stroke was due . . . . he

poured out his soul unto death . . . . And they made his grave with the wicked. . . . (53:8,12,9)

f) The Servant of Jehovah is the great sin bearer and intercessor:

. . . he bare the sin of many, and made intercession for the transgressors. (53:12)

But the death of the Servant of Jehovah was predetermined by God to become the means of man's redemption:

. . . and Jehovah hath laid on him the iniquity of us all. . . . Yet it pleased Jehovah to bruise him; he hath put him to grief: when thou shalt make his soul an offering for sin, he shall see his seed, he shall prolong his days, and the pleasure [or purpose] of Jehovah shall prosper in his hand. (53:6,10)

So far, the picture of the Messianic Person has been one of suffering and death, but a completely different portrait is drawn in other Old Testament Scriptures. The Prophet Jeremiah states that he is Israel's King and that he is also a God-Man, that is, God becoming a man:

Behold, the days come, saith Jehovah, that I will raise unto David a righteous Branch, and he shall reign as king and deal wisely, and shall execute justice and righteousness in the land. In his days Judah shall be saved, and Israel shall dwell safely; and this is his name whereby he shall be called: Jehovah our righteousness. (23:5-6)

As can be seen from these two verses, this Messianic Person is to be a king of the Davidic dynasty and will go by the name of "Jehovah our righteousness." A mere man would never be called Jehovah by a Jewish prophet. But if God chose to become a man, and God most certainly has the power to do so, then that man could be called Jehovah. The same idea of God becoming a man is stated in the book of Isaiah:

> For unto us a child is born, unto us a son is given; and the government shall be upon his shoulder: and his name shall be called Wonderful, Counsellor, Mighty God, Everlasting Father, Prince of Peace. (9:6)

A child is born, yet names are given to him which can only be applicable to God. Another Scripture relating to this Messianic Person and which shows his qualifications for his mission is Isaiah 11:2-10:

> And the Spirit of Jehovah shall rest upon him, the spirit of wisdom and understanding, the spirit of counsel and might, the spirit of knowledge and of the fear of Jehovah; and his delight shall be in the fear of Jehovah; and he shall not judge after the sight of his eyes, neither decide after the hearing of his ears; but with righteousness shall he judge the poor, and decide with equity for the meek of the earth; and he shall smite the earth with the rod of his mouth, and with the breath of his lips shall he slay the wicked. And righteousness shall be the girdle of his waist, and faithfulness the girdle of his loins.
>
> And the wolf shall dwell with the lamb, and the leopard shall lie down with the kid; and the calf and the young lion and the fatling together; and a little child shall lead them. And the cow and the bear shall feed; their young ones shall lie down together; and the lion shall eat straw like the ox. And the sucking child shall play on the hole of the asp, and the weaned child shall put his hand on the adder's den. They shall not hurt nor destroy in all my holy mountain; for the earth shall be full of the knowledge of Jehovah, as the waters cover the sea.
>
> And it shall come to pass in that day, that the root of Jesse, that standeth for an ensign of the peoples, unto him shall the nations seek; and his resting-place shall be glorious.

The thrust of this passage is that the Messianic Program will be headed up by the Messianic Person. The wicked are to be judged and world peace achieved, not by force, but by the transformation of human nature and world-wide diffusion of the knowledge of Jehovah.

What is all this saying? It is saying that the Messianic Person was required to come twice to this sinful world. At his first coming as the suffering Servant of Jehovah, recorded in Isaiah 53 and other passages, his purpose was to die and by his death pay the penalty for sin. Through the power of his resurrection all can receive the new birth (that is, a new life in fellowship with God) simply by accepting him as the Messiah. Individual Jews and individual Gentiles who accept Jesus as Messiah become believers, or Christians. We Hebrew Christians believe that Jesus is this Messianic Person and that he will complete his Messianic Program at his second coming.

THE MESSIANIC PEOPLE

The third of these three lines is a *Messianic People*. We Hebrew Christians believe that Israel is the Messianic People and that their mission is to win the Gentile nations to God under the direction of the Messianic Person. This selection of Israel is described in the Old Testament by Isaiah:

> The people which I formed for myself, that they might set forth my praise. (43:21)

Furthermore, God said to his ancient people through Moses:

> Ye have seen what I did unto the Egyptians, and how I bare you on eagles' wings, and brought you unto myself. Now therefore, if ye will obey my voice indeed, and keep my covenant, then ye shall be mine own possession from among all peoples: for all the earth is mine: and ye shall be unto me a kingdom of priests, and a holy nation. (Exodus 19:4-6)

God is the creator of all things, and this includes all nations. Israel along with every other nation forms part of God's possessions; but God has chosen Israel to be his own in a special degree, to be a light unto the Gentiles and a blessing to all humanity.

More will be said concerning the Messianic People in the next chapter.

Conclusion

In conclusion it should be noted that some parts of these three lines of Messianism have been fulfilled but that other parts are awaiting the second coming of Messiah. For we believe that Jesus is the Messiah who will return and accomplish what has been prophesied of him. He is the Messianic Person who will direct the Messianic People in accomplishing the Messianic Program. Jesus the Messiah, when he returns, will become the king of the nation of Israel.

CHAPTER V

HEBREW CHRISTIANITY
AND THE JEWS

The relationship between the Hebrew Christian and the un-believing Jewish community is one of paradoxes. He considers himself a member of the Jewish community but is not consid-ered one by his fellow Jews. He is extremely loyal to the Jews and yet is considered by them to be a traitor. He is the most effective fighter of anti-Semitism but is accused by the Jews of being anti-Semitic. The list of paradoxes can easily be extended, but the basic cause of them all is misunderstanding on the part of the Jewish community concerning exactly where the Hebrew Christian stands. While the Hebrew Christian is very definite about what constitutes Jewishness, the Jewish community is not. While the Hebrew Christian knows what the differences are between Gentiles and Christians, the Jewish community does not. Furthermore, he is also clear on what part the Mes-sianic People play in world history and in God's program, while there is no such clear concept in the Jewish community. The Hebrew Christian's understanding of the exact role of the Messianic People in world history produces within him a loyalty to the Jews causing him to defend them against all attacks. The purpose of this chapter is to outline the Hebrew Christian's position on and his attitude towards the Messianic People in their role in history.

The Abrahamic Covenant

Much has already been said about the Abrahamic Covenant,

but we have hardly exhausted all the implications involved in it. The development of the Messianic People in history is based on this covenant, which is found in Genesis 12:1-3:

> Now Jehovah said unto Abram, Get thee out of thy country, and from thy kindred, and from thy father's house, unto the land that I will show thee: and I will make of thee a great nation, and I will bless thee, and make thy name great; and be thou a blessing: and I will bless them that bless thee, and him that curseth thee will I curse: and in thee shall all the families of the earth be blessed.

As we have seen, in this covenant God is essentially promising Abraham three things: first, that from him will come forth a people or a nation; second, to this nation God will give a land; and third, God will bless those who bless this nation and curse those who curse it. In this chapter it is the third point with which we are concerned: "I will bless them that bless thee, and him that curseth thee will I curse."

Very early in human history a principle was set down to control the relationship of the Jews with the Gentiles. Politically speaking we could call this statement God's foreign policy to the Gentiles in their relationship with the Jewish people. It is restated in wider terms in Deuteronomy 32:8-9:

> When the Most High gave to the nations their inheritance,
> When he separated the children of men,
> He set the bounds of the peoples
> According to the number of the children of Israel.
> For Jehovah's portion is his people;
> Jacob is the lot of his inheritance.

It is not only God's program for Israel that centers around the Jews, but his program for the Gentiles as well; when God in his providence sets down boundaries for the Gentile nations, he somehow takes into account the number of the Jews.

The history of philosophy is simply the retracing and reviewing of the ways man has tried to explain his being, knowledge, and other areas with which philosophy is concerned. The philosophy of history, however, tries to extract principles from history by which history can be understood and provide a prospectus of how history will develop in the future. In the Abrahamic Covenant we have such a principle: those who bless the Jews will be blessed and those who curse them will be cursed. Understanding this principle will help to explain much in history that cannot be explained any other way.

Now we will take the Scriptures and see how this principle works itself out both on the individual and national levels in relation to the Jews. We will also see how it affects the lives of Gentile individuals and nations.

The Outworking of the Abrahamic Covenant on the Individual Level

To begin, let us observe how the Abrahamic Covenant works itself out in the lives of individual Jews. Once the covenant is given, it begins to operate immediately:

> And there was a famine in the land: and Abram went down into Egypt to sojourn there; for the famine was sore in the land. And it came to pass, when he was come near to enter into Egypt, that he said to Sarai his wife, Behold now, I know that thou art a fair woman to look upon: and it will come to pass, when the Egyptians shall see thee, that they will say, This is his wife: and they will kill me, but they will save thee alive. Say, I pray thee, thou art my sister; that it may be well with me for thy sake, and that my soul may live because of thee. And it came to pass, when Abram was come into Egypt, the Egyptians beheld the woman that she was very fair. And the princes of Pharaoh saw her, and praised her to Pharaoh: and the woman was taken into Pharaoh's house. (Genesis 12:10-15)

If anyone can be said to be at fault here, it is certainly not the king of Egypt. Abraham comes into Egypt telling a half-truth with the result that Sarah is taken from him and put into Pharaoh's harem. At least once in the long relationship between the Jews and Egyptians, the Egyptians were not at fault. At least this once. Nevertheless, in the outworking of the Abrahamic Covenant God begins to operate on Abraham's behalf; so in verse seventeen we read:

> And Jehovah plagued Pharaoh and his house with great plagues because of Sarai, Abram's wife.

We see the same thing happening all over again in Genesis 20:1-2, only a different country and a different king are involved:

> And Abraham journeyed from thence toward the land of the South, and dwelt between Kadesh and Shur; and he sojourned in Gerar. And Abraham said of Sarah his wife, She is my sister: and Abimelech king of Gerar sent, and took Sarah.

Once again the same half-truth, half-lie is told. Once again the result is the same; Sarah is taken from him. Again in the outworking of the Abrahamic Covenant God begins to operate on Abraham's behalf. In verse three we read:

> But God came to Abimelech in a dream of the night, and said to him, Behold, thou art but a dead man, because of the woman whom thou hast taken; for she is a man's wife.

The above two passages perhaps indicate the first real attempt to destroy the Jews. For God had already promised that he would bless the Gentiles through the Jews and that the Jews would continue through Abraham's son Isaac. Now both of these incidents occurred before Isaac was born, and I see here a definite attempt to keep Isaac from being born by taking his future mother away. If Satan could keep Isaac from being born, then the Jews would die out with the death of Abraham. Unknowingly, Abimelech cursed Abraham in such a way as to destroy the Jews, and now God curses Abimelech. When God operates on the cursing aspect of the Abrahamic Covenant, he works on the sub-principle of *curse for curse in kind*. The specific type of curse used against the Jews will be used against the curser. This is seen in verse eighteen of this chapter:

> For Jehovah had fast closed up all the wombs of the house of Abimelech, because of Sarah, Abraham's wife.

It was now the house of Abimelech that faced possible extinction because of the inability of the women in his household to give birth. After Abraham prayed for Abimelech upon the latter's restoring Sarah, the curse was lifted. This first attempt to destroy the Jews failed, and Isaac was born as recorded in the following chapter.

Just as the cursing aspect of the Abrahamic Covenant had begun to operate on the individual level, so did the blessing aspect. This is seen in the life of Jacob in Genesis 30:25-30:

> And it came to pass, when Rachel had borne Joseph, that Jacob said unto Laban, Send me away, that I may go unto mine own place, and to my country. Give me my wives and my children for whom I have served thee, and let me go: for thou knowest my service wherewith I have served thee. And Laban said unto him, If now I have found favor in thine eyes, tarry: for I have divined that Jehovah hath blessed me for thy sake. And he said, Appoint me thy wages, and I will give it. And he said unto him. Thou knowest how I have served thee, and how thy cattle have fared with me. For it was little which thou hadst before I came, and it hath increased into a multitude; and Jehovah hath blessed thee whithersoever I turned: and now when shall I provide for mine own household also?

At the outset one thing should be made very clear. Laban was no worshipper of the true God. He worshipped many gods and had many idols. So when his nephew Jacob came bringing the God Jehovah, Laban, a very ecumenical individual, was very happy to include Jehovah among his many other gods as well. Nevertheless, this pagan recognized something; he recognized that this God of Jacob, whoever he was, was blessing him because of his relationship with Jacob the Jew. So to the oft-repeated question of whether God can bless the ungodly, the answer is yes. There are some blessings of God which are determined by the spiritual status of the one blessed. But there are others which are conditioned on other matters. The blessings of the Abrahamic Covenant are based purely on the relationship with the Jews. So Laban the pagan was blessed because he had a proper relationship with Jacob the Jew.

Another example of the blessing aspect of this covenant is found in Genesis 39:1-5:

> And Joseph was brought down to Egypt; and Potiphar, an officer of Pharaoh's, the captain of the guard, an Egyptian, bought him of the hand of the Ishmaelites, that had brought him down thither. And Jehovah was with Joseph, and he was a prosperous man; and he was in the house of his master the Egyptian. And his master saw that Jehovah was with him, and that Jehovah made all that he did to prosper in his hand. And Joseph found favor in his sight, and he ministered unto him: and he made him overseer over his house, and all that he had he put into his hand. And it came to pass from the time that he made him overseer in his house, and over all that he had, that Jehovah blessed the Egyptian's house for Joseph's sake; and the blessing of Jehovah was upon all that he had, in the house and in the field.

Once again we see God blessing a pagan, an Egyptian, because of his proper relationship with Joseph the Jew.

The book of Genesis is, among other things, a record of the outworking of the Abrahamic Covenant on the individual level. God's philosophy of history has begun to operate on the principle of blessing those who bless the Jews and cursing in kind those who curse them.

The Outworking of the Abrahamic Covenant on the National Level

When we come to the book of Exodus, we begin dealing with the national level of God's philosophy of history; that is, we now deal with Israel as a nation rather than with individual Jews. In the first chapter of the book of Exodus, Egypt sets out to curse Israel. The curse is in two phases. The first is found in Exodus 1:8-11:

> Now there arose a new king over Egypt, who knew not Joseph. And he said unto his people, Behold, the people of the children of Israel are more and mightier than we: come, let us deal wisely with them, lest they multiply, and it come to pass, that, when there falleth out any war, they also join themselves unto our enemies, and fight against us, and get them up out of the land. Therefore they did set over them taskmasters to afflict them with their burdens. And they built for Pharaoh store-cities, Pithom and Raamses.

Egypt has a unique distinction. She is the first nation that can be called truly anti-Semitic in the modern sense of the term. In the first phase of her curse against Israel she puts the Jews into slavery. But after a while this is not enough, and so a second phase is initiated:

> And the king of Egypt spake to the Hebrew midwives, of whom the name of the one was Shiphrah, and the name of the other Puah: and he said, When ye do the office of a midwife to the Hebrew women, and see them upon the birth-stool; if it be a son, then ye shall kill him; but if it be a daughter, then she shall live. . . . And Pharaoh charged all his people, saying, Every son that is born ye shall cast into the river, and every daughter ye shall save alive. (1:15-16,22)

Not only is Egypt the first anti-Semitic nation, she is the first nation to attempt genocide against the Jews. So now in this second phase she is out to destroy the new-born sons by means of drowning.

Now God waits and he waits. He waits four hundred years before delivering his people. Yet another sub-principle involved in the Abrahamic Covenant is that sometimes God will delay a long time before keeping his promise to the Jews, but sooner or later that promise will be kept. Finally, after four hundred years, God begins to work, and again we see the sub-principle of curse for curse in kind:

> And thou shalt say unto Pharaoh, Thus saith Jehovah, Israel is my son, my first-born: and I have said unto thee, Let my son go, that he may serve me; and thou hast refused to let him go: behold, I will slay thy son, thy first-born. (Exodus 4:22-23)

The curse against Israel was to kill the new-born sons. Now God sends ten plagues upon Egypt, the last resulting in the death of every first-born Egyptian son. As Israel leaves Egypt and the Egyptian army chases in hot pursuit, God destroys the Egyptian army by means of drowning. It is curse for curse in kind.

But no sooner does Israel leave Egypt than another nation comes to curse the Jews. In Exodus 17:8 we read:

> Then came Amalek, and fought with Israel in Rephidim.

The method used here to destroy the Jews is war. So in return God curses Amalek:

> And Jehovah said unto Moses, Write this for a memorial in a book, and rehearse it in the ears of Joshua: that I will utterly blot out the remembrance of Amalek from under heaven. And Moses built an altar, and called the name of it Jehovah-nissi; and he said, Jehovah hath sworn: Jehovah will have war with Amalek from generation to generation. (Exodus 17:14-16)

Amalek declared war on Israel and now God declares war on Amalek. Once again God waits about four hundred years, until Israel receives her first king, before he does anything about bringing the war to its end:

> And Samuel said unto Saul, Jehovah sent me to anoint thee to be king over his people, over Israel: now therefore hearken thou unto the voice of the words of Jehovah. Thus saith Jehovah of hosts, I have marked that which Amalek did to Israel, how he set himself against him in the way, when he came up out of Egypt. Now go and smite Amalek, and utterly destroy all that they have, and spare them not; but slay both man and woman, infant and suckling, ox and sheep, camel and ass. (I Samuel 15:1-3)

Although the crime was committed four hundred years earlier, God nevertheless had marked it down, and now the first king of Israel is ordered to bring the war to a close. But when Saul goes out he runs into a problem. When Amalek cursed Israel four centuries earlier, another group called the Kenites had blessed them. By this time these Kenites were living among the Amalekites, but of course they were not under the curse. The problem is solved by a delay in the attack:

> And Saul came to the city of Amalek, and laid wait in the valley. And Saul said unto the Kenites, Go, depart, get you down from among the Amalekites, lest I destroy you with them; for ye showed kindness to all the children of Israel, when they came up out of Egypt. So the Kenites departed from among the Amalekites. (I Samuel 15:5-6)

In these two passages from I Samuel we can see how the Abrahamic Covenant worked itself out in the lives of two nations both in its blessing and cursing aspects. Another attempt to destroy the Jews failed.

One book in the Scriptures that portrays beautifully the outworking of the Abrahamic Covenant is the book of Esther. This book has one very unusual feature about it. Try as you may, you will not find in it a single reference to God. There is no mention

of him, no prayer to him, nothing. In fact, a careful reading of
the book of Esther will show that it is going out of its way to
avoid mentioning him. So when Mordecai argues with Esther
about trying to save the Jews, he says, "For if thou altogether
holdest thy peace at this time, then will relief and deliverance
arise to the Jews from another place . . ." (4:14). All Mordecai
says is "another place." He does not mention the word "God."
Such a statement indicates that the writer is purposely abstain-
ing from using the word. If this is true, then what is this book
doing in the Scriptures? Just this: although God is not mentioned, we see him working. But God is not working in just any
old way; he is working specifically according to the Abrahamic
Covenant.

In this book a man by the name of Haman sets out with his
curse against the Jews:

> After these things did king Ahasuerus promote Haman the
> son of Hammedatha the Agagite, and advanced him, and set
> his seat above all the princes that were with him. And all the
> king's servants, that were in the king's gate, bowed down, and
> did reverence to Haman; for the king had so commanded
> concerning him. But Mordecai bowed not down, nor did him
> reverence. . . . And when Haman saw that Mordecai bowed not
> down, nor did him reverence, then was Haman full of wrath.
> But he thought scorn to lay hands on Mordecai alone; for they
> had made known to him the people of Mordecai: Wherefore
> Haman sought to destroy all the Jews that were throughout the
> whole kingdom of Ahasuerus, even the people of Mordecai.
> (Esther 3:1-2,5-6)

So because one Jew will not bend his knees to him, Haman
is so angry that he wants to destroy all the Jews in the Persian
Empire. His method is described in 3:12-13:

> Then were the king's scribes called in the first month, on the
> thirteenth day thereof; and there was written according to all
> that Haman commanded unto the king's satraps, and to the
> governors that were over every province, and to the princes of

every people, to every province according to the writing thereof, and to every people after their language; in the name of king Ahasuerus was it written, and it was sealed with the king's ring. And letters were sent by posts into all the king's provinces, to destroy, to slay, and to cause to perish, all Jews, both young and old, little children and women, in one day, even upon the thirteeth day of the twelfth month, which is the month of Adar, and to take the spoil of them for a prey.

Haman seeks to destroy the Jews by making anti-Semitism the official government policy. He issues a decree stating that on a certain day of a certain month anyone who wants to may kill a Jew and suffer no legal penalties for it. In fact, the law now encourages the killing of Jews. This decree is signed with the king's ring and sent out to the whole bureaucracy of the Persian Empire. Under Persian jurisprudence, once a decree was so signed it could never be repealed. Not even the emperor of Persia himself had the authority to repeal a decree that was sealed with his own ring. Therefore this decree making Jews fair game can never be repealed. And so it stands.

One would think that this would make our anti-Semite happy. But it doesn't. He wants special treatment for Mordecai, the one who made him angry in the first place, but he does not know how to handle the situation. So he receives advice from his wife:

> Yet all this availeth me nothing, so long as I see Mordecai the Jew sitting at the king's gate. Then said Zeresh his wife and all his friends unto him, Let a gallows be made fifty cubits high, and in the morning speak thou unto the king that Mordecai may be hanged thereon: then go thou in merrily with the king unto the banquet. And the thing pleased Haman; and he caused the gallows to be made. (5:13-14)

The simple counsel of his wife is followed, and Haman goes to bed waiting for the morning when he can ask the king for Mordecai's head.

Chapter six opens with an incident that is happening the same night the gallows are being built:

> On that night could not the king sleep; and he commanded to bring the book of records of the chronicles, and they were read before the king. (6:1)

Sometime before this fateful night, Mordecai had saved the king's life (Esther 2:21-23). Although neither the king nor Haman knew about this, some faithful scribe had recorded it in the chronicles of the Persian Empire. When chapter six quietly opens with the words "on that night," contained in those three words is the beginning of the work of God on the basis of the Abrahamic Covenant.

As the scribe reads to the king from the chronicles, he soon comes to the account of Mordecai's deed. This is the first time the king has heard about it, and he wants to know if Mordecai has been rewarded. The answer is no. At this time Haman comes in to ask for Mordecai's head. But before he has a chance to make his request, the king asks a question first:

> So Haman came in. And the king said unto him, What shall be done unto the man whom the king delighteth to honor? Now Haman said in his heart, To whom would the king delight to do honor more than to myself? (6:6)

What is to be done for the man whom the king wants to honor? This simple question causes a response in the mind of Haman: who could the king possibly want to honor other than him? Haman's humility is beginning to show through! So, believing that he is the one the king wants to reward, he proceeds to ask for the king's horse, the king's clothes, and the king's crown. Very humble gifts. But these are not all. These things are to be delivered to the one Haman calls "one of the king's most noble princes," which happens to be Haman's chief competitor. This competitor is then to dress Haman in these clothes, put him on the horse, and lead him through the main street of the city shouting, "Thus shall it be done to the man whom the king delighteth to honor."

Having said all this, Haman is ready and primed to hear the words "Thou art the man." Upon those words he was intending to fake a surprised look.

> Then the king said to Haman, Make haste, and take the apparel and the horse, as thou hast said, and do even so to Mordecai the Jew, that sitteth at the king's gate: let nothing fail of all that thou hast spoken. (6:10)

The surprised look on Haman's face was not faked. God had begun to operate by humbling Haman. But in the end it is curse for curse in kind; in Esther 7:9-10 we read:

> Then said Harbonah, one of the chamberlains that were before the king, Behold also, the gallows fifty cubits high, which Haman hath made for Mordecai, who spake good for the king, standeth in the house of Haman. And the king said, Hang him thereon. So they hanged Haman on the gallows that he had prepared for Mordecai. Then was the king's wrath pacified.

But even with Haman dead, swinging on the gallows meant for Mordecai, the problem was not solved. A decree had been passed which could never be repealed; the Jews were still fair game whenever that certain day of the certain month arrived. Since the decree could not be repealed, a second one was passed, also sealed with the king's ring, which stated that on the same day of that same month the Jews would be free to take up weapons to defend themselves (Esther 8:9-14).

> And the Jews smote all their enemies with the stroke of the sword, and with slaughter and destruction, and did what they would unto them that hated them. (Esther 9:5)

Again we see the sub-principle of curse for curse in kind. The grand finale of the whole episode is a new Jewish holiday which is still celebrated today:

Wherefore they called these days Purim, after the name of Pur. (9:26)

The chief propagandist for the Hitler regime was Julias Streicher, who through his Nazi newspaper spread Jew-hatred all over Europe. After World War II he was captured by the Allied Forces, tried at Nuremburg, and sentenced to be hung. As he went up the scaffold he spoke his two last words, "Purim—1946." Julias Streicher recognized the part he played in history. He tried to destroy the Jews, but now in the closing minutes of his life he realized that the Jews he had tried to destroy would celebrate his failure as they have Haman's.

THE OUTWORKING OF THE ABRAHAMIC COVENANT IN THE NEW TESTAMENT

The New Testament demonstrates the continuity of the Abrahamic Covenant and the principle of God's philosophy of history. An example of this is found in Luke 7:2-5:

> And a certain centurion's servant, who was dear unto him, was sick and at the point of death. And when he heard concerning Jesus, he sent unto him elders of the Jews, asking him that he would come and save his servant. And they, when they came to Jesus, besought him earnestly, saying, He is worthy that thou shouldest do this for him; for he loveth our nation, and himself built us our synagogue.

At this time in history the Romans were not friends of the Jews. But there was something different about this particular Roman. The Jewish leaders themselves testified that he "loveth our nation, and himself built us our synagogue." So in the outworking of the blessing aspect of the Abrahamic Covenant, we read in verse ten:

> And they that were sent, returning to the house, found the servant whole.

A second example involves another Roman centurion. In Acts chapter ten, the first Gentile as a Gentile, rather than as a proselyte, is received into the church. It should be noted that of all the Gentiles God could have chosen as the first to come into the Body of Christ, he picked one that was "a righteous man and one that feareth God, and well reported of by all the nation of the Jews . . ." (Acts 10:22a).

Throughout the Scriptures, we see over and over again the blessing and cursing aspects of the Abrahamic Covenant among the Gentiles, both as individuals and as nations, in their relationship with the Jews.

THE OUTWORKING OF THE ABRAHAMIC COVENANT IN POST-BIBLICAL HISTORY

Many events in history that are labeled peculiar and unusual or impossible to understand can best be understood if viewed as a result of the outworking of the Abrahamic Covenant. There have been numerous attempts to destroy the Jews, and all have failed. Essentially, the same four methods that were used during the biblical period have been the same ones used ever since, and these methods will always fail in destroying the Jews. Like Abimelech, the Crusaders took away the wives. Like the Egyptians, the Spanish Empire killed the sons. Like the Persian Empire, Germany made anti-Semitism the official government policy. Like the Amalekites, the Arab states have declared war upon the Jews. These methods cannot and will not work in destroying them.

After two thousand years, numerous examples could be given of how the Abrahamic Covenant has worked itself out, but we will limit ourselves to four.

Because of its great Armada, the Spanish Empire controlled vast parts of the world. The fact that every nation south of the United States, except Brazil, speaks Spanish is an indication of what the Spanish Empire once was. The Spanish economy was strong, and as a result so was everything else. In 1492, the same year Columbus set sail for America, the Spanish Edict of Expulsion was issued ordering all Jews to leave the country. With this act Spain blundered. When she expelled her Jews, she expelled her scholars, doctors, and bankers. The Spanish economy thus began to crumble and collapse. Finally, the source of Spain's strength, the Armada, sailed against England and was destroyed, not so much by the British navy as by a storm at sea. The Abrahamic Covenant had worked itself out. She who expelled the Jews was then expelled from her holdings in the Western Hemisphere until nothing remained.

Another point involving Spain shows the blessing aspect beginning to work as well. The story of how Queen Isabella sold her jewels in order to buy the three ships for Columbus breaks down under some cool historical research. It was not Queen Isabella's jewels, but Queen Isabella's Jews who purchased the three ships for Columbus. History shows that two Jewish banking families bought the ships. Many of the men on the three vessels were Jews fleeing Spain as a result of the Edict of Expulsion. According to Columbus's own diary, the first one to spot land was a Jew sitting in the crow's nest. Also, according to his diary, the first one off his ship was his interpreter, Louis de Tores, a Spanish Jew. So as Europe was slowly beginning to close its doors to the Jews, a new world was discovered that was eventually to become, in the form of the United States, the greatest haven for Jews fleeing persecution around the world. The United States became and remains what she is today mainly because of the blessing aspect of the Abrahamic Covenant.

England provides a second example of the outworking of the Abrahamic Covenant. There was a time when England was blessed by God because of her favorable attitude to the Jews, and they were able to boast: "The sun never sets on the British Empire." It was a Hebrew Christian, Benjamin Disraeli, who gained for England the two vital links which made her the

British Empire, India and the Suez Canal. The Balfour Declaration in World War I showed England's favorable attitude towards establishing a Jewish national home in Palestine, which was later captured from the Turks. But then she made an about-face and turned against the Jews. In effect disannulling the Balfour Declaration, England began to limit Jewish immigration. This policy trapped many Jews, preventing their flight from the Nazis. As a result the British Empire also began to crumble as one nation after another declared its freedom from the Empire. Finally, the very possessions gained for her by Jews, India and the Suez Canal, were also lost. The result is that today the sun does indeed set on the British Empire, every twenty-four hours.

Germany provides us with the third example. When Hitler came to power, anti-Semitism became the official government policy. As the Germans in 1939 drew the world into war, this policy began to spread to the occupied parts of Europe. As one nation after another fell, the Jews were taken and moved into slum sections of major cities, such as Warsaw. Concrete walls were built around these ghettos, and the Jews were slowly beaten and starved. The Gestapo had a favorite game which consisted of taking one Jew and forcing him to kill another Jew in order to save the life of his own family. Jews were forced to go into hiding as Nazis systematically sought them out. Six million were finally exterminated.

But after six years Germany was no longer the conqueror but the conquered. The Germans, who once built walls around the Jews, now have a wall cutting in half their once proud capitol Berlin. The people who once forced Jews to kill Jews now have Germans killing Germans who try to make their escape over the Berlin Wall. To this day Nazi criminals are forced to live in hiding as Jews seek them out. All this provides us with a unique picture of the sub-principle of curse for curse in kind.

The fourth example involves the four Arab states of Syria, Iraq, Jordan, and Egypt, all of whom combined their forces in

1967 with the avowed purpose of destroying Israel. Nasser vowed that the Jews would be driven into the Mediterranean Sea and forced to swim back to Europe, from where they came. King Hussein swore to move his border so as to encompass all of Palestine. After four days of the Six Day War, however, it was not the Jews but the Egyptians who were doing the swimming as they fled across the Suez Canal from the Israeli forces. As for King Hussein, after three days his border was indeed moved, but in the opposite direction. The Arabs cursed the Jewish state with war and were defeated by war.

The philosophy of history involved in the Abrahamic Covenant provides the principles for understanding how the Gentile nations are related to the Jews.

THE OUTWORKING OF THE ABRAHAMIC COVENANT
IN PROPHECY

In order to provide a somewhat complete picture of the Abrahamic covenant two examples will be cited from the realm of eschatology.

At the time of this writing the main persecutor of the Jews is the Soviet Union. She is troubling the Jews inside her territory and is allied with the Arab states in their stated aim to destroy the state of Israel. But the Scriptures in Ezekiel 38:1-39:16 have already declared how the Soviet Union will come to its end.[1] A full exposition of this passage goes beyond the scope of this book except to say that the very event which begins the work of God against the Russians is depicted in Ezekiel 38:18:

> And it shall come to pass in that day, when Gog shall come against the land of Israel, saith the Lord Jehovah, that my wrath shall come up into my nostrils.

The final straw will be when the Russians themselves invade

1. The author is aware of differences in interpretation of this passage. For differing points of view cf. D. Guthrie et al., eds., *The New Bible Commentary: Revised* (Grand Rapids: Eerdmans, 1970), pp. 681-682; and J. Barton Payne, *Encyclopedia of Biblical Prophecy* (New York: Harper & Row, 1973), p. 367.

the nation of Israel; having done that, the Russians as a world power are doomed.

The second example is the campaign of Armageddon resulting in the second coming of Messiah. Again, a complete exposition on Armageddon goes beyond the purpose of this chapter except to note that the event which actually begins God's action against the Gentiles in this campaign is recorded by Zechariah:

> Behold, I will make Jerusalem a cup of reeling unto all the peoples round about, and upon Judah also shall it be in the siege against Jerusalem. And it shall come to pass in that day, that I will make Jerusalem a burdensome stone for all the peoples; all that burden themselves with it shall be sore wounded; and all the nations of the earth shall be gathered together against it. (12:2-3)

> Behold, a day of Jehovah cometh, when thy spoil shall be divided in the midst of thee. For I will gather all nations against Jerusalem to battle; and the city shall be taken, and the houses rifled, and the women ravished; and half of the city shall go forth into captivity, and the residue of the people shall not be cut off from the city. Then shall Jehovah go forth, and fight against those nations, as when he fought in the day of battle. And his feet shall stand in that day upon the mount of Olives, which is before Jerusalem on the east; and the mount of Olives shall be cleft in the midst thereof toward the east and toward the west, and there shall be a very great valley; and half of the mountain shall remove toward the north, and half of it toward the south. (14:1-4)

Thus in prophecy as well as in history the unifying principle is the Abrahamic Covenant. The occurrence that brings the present dispensation to its end is the gathering against Jerusalem of all the Gentile nations. This will bring about the second coming of Christ.

CONCLUSION

Books on Jewish history written from a secular viewpoint are generally agreed that Jewish existence is an enigma. Historians with different philosophies of history, such as Oswald Spengler and Arnold Toynbee, find themselves at a loss to explain the Jews. This is pointed out by Max I. Dimont in *Jews, God and History*:

> Since the history of the Jews did not fit into either Spengler's or Toynbee's system, Spengler ignored them and Toynbee reduced them to an occasional footnote, describing the Jews as fossils of history.[2]

Philosophies of history based on non-biblical presuppositions fail to provide any answer to Jewish survival. This is clear from the very writings of those who tried to explain history by a certain system only to have it crack down in the face of the Jews. Mark Twain wrote in "Concerning the Jews":

> He could be vain of himself, and be excused for it. The Egyptian, the Babylonian, and the Persian rose, filled the planet with sound and splendor, then faded to dream-stuff and passed away; the Greek and the Roman followed, and made a vast noise, and they are gone; other peoples have sprung up and held their torch high for a time, but it burned out, and they sit in twilight, or have vanished. The Jew saw them all, beat them all, and is now what he always was, exhibiting no decadence, no infirmities of age, no weakening of his parts, no slowing of his energies, no dulling of his alert and aggressive mind. All things are mortal but the Jew; all other forces pass, but he remains. What is the secret of his immortality?[3]

A former communist by the name of Nicholas Berdyaev writes in *The Meaning of History*:

> I remember how the materialist interpretation of history, when I attempted in my youth to verify it by applying it to the

2. Max I. Dimont, *Jews, God and History* (New York: The New American Library, Inc., 1962), p. 20.

3. Mark Twain, "Concerning the Jews" in *The Man That Corrupted Hadleyburg and Other Stories and Essays* (New York: Harper & Bros., 1900), p. 281.

destinies of the people, broke down in the case of the Jews, where destiny seemed absolutely inexplicable from the materialistic standpoint.... According to the materialistic ... criterion, this people ought long ago to have perished. Its survival is a mysterious and wonderful phenomenon demonstrating that the life of this people is governed by a special predetermination, transcending the processes of adaptation expounded by the materialistic interpretation of history. The survival of the Jews ... their endurance under absolutely peculiar conditions and the fateful role played by them in history; all these point to the peculiar and mysterious foundations of their destiny.[4]

Not only have Gentile historians, looking at the Jews, come to a dead end in trying to explain them, but the Jews themselves have not been able to explain their existence in any consistent way. But the Hebrew Christian has the answer to the secret of Jewish survival. The answer to Mark Twain's question, "What is the secret of his immortality?" lies in the outworking of the Abrahamic Covenant. The answer lies in this cry of the last of the Old Testament prophets:

> For I, Jehovah, change not; therefore ye, O sons of Jacob, are not consumed. (Malachi 3:6)

The Hebrew Christian, then, can give the proper explanation of the role the Messianic People play in history. Their destruction is impossible. It is true that great parts of the Messianic People have been destroyed through various anti-Semitic campaigns, but the Messianic People as a distinct entity cannot themselves be destroyed. The Hebrew Christian, being part of the Messianic People, enjoys the same protection. The difference is in their knowing the source of that protection.

Thus the Hebrew Christian is a loyal member of the Jewish community, although the community may not accept him. Knowing the exact nature of God's program for the Messianic People draws him to a greater love for his own people in a way

4. Nicholas Berdyaev, *The Meaning of History* (London: Geoffrey Bles, Centenary Press, 1936), pp. 86-87.

that most Jews cannot understand. His desire to share the truths of the Scriptures with them is the result of his love for the Jews and not the result of any antagonism towards them.

On the other hand, the Hebrew Christian's alliance with the Jews does not make him blind to the fact that the Jewish community is not always right. Nor does it blind him to the fact that the basic cause of Jewish suffering is their disobedience to the revealed will of God and unbelief in the person of the Messiah. These things are countered by witnessing to the Jews. At the same time he is the best defender of the Jews against all forms of anti-Semitism, teaching God's attitude towards it and warning of God's judgment if it persists.

For the anti-Semite who cannot be persuaded by the Scriptures to drop his anti-Semitism, the Hebrew Christian has some useful information. The anti-Semite can be told that it will not work to take Jewish wives away, to kill Jewish sons, to declare war on the Jews, or to make anti-Semitism the official government policy. These four methods consistently used against the Jews throughout history cannot and will not destroy them. The Hebrew Christian can provide the one method that will work in destroying the Jews. It is found in Jeremiah 31:35-37:

> Thus saith Jehovah, who giveth the sun for a light by day, and the ordinances of the moon and of the stars for a light by night, who stirreth up the sea, so that the waves thereof roar; Jehovah of hosts is his name: If these ordinances depart from before me, saith Jehovah, then the seed of Israel also shall cease from being a nation before me for ever. Thus saith Jehovah: If heaven above can be measured, and the foundations of the earth searched out beneath, then will I also cast off all the seed of Israel for all that they have done, saith Jehovah.

The message of the Hebrew Christian to the anti-Semite is: If you want to destroy the Jews, then you must first destroy the sun, moon, and stars; then, and only then, according to the promise of God, can the Jews be destroyed.

CHAPTER VI

THE LAW OF MOSES

If there is one immediate problem that seems to face the new Jewish believer in Christ, it is his relationship to the Law of Moses. This is more of a problem to the Hebrew Christian in Israel than to his counterpart in the United States, but every Hebrew Christian faces it to some measure. If I could generalize for a moment, I would say that the average American Hebrew Christian concurs with a partial keeping of the Law while the average Israeli believer concurs with the keeping of all of it, excluding those parts dealing with the Temple and its functions. But regardless of the extent, the dilemma is the same: to what extent is the Hebrew Christian to keep the Law of Moses?

Two factors have developed in the minds and teachings of many Christians which have contributed to the creation of this problem. One is the practice of dividing the Law into ceremonial, legal, and moral commandments. On the basis of this division many have come to think that the believer is free from the ceremonial and legal commandments but is still under the moral commandments. The second factor is the belief that the Ten Commandments are still valid today while the other 603 commandments are not. When confronted by a Seventh Day Adventist, the individual taking this approach runs into problems concerning the fourth commandment on keeping the Sabbath. At that point fudging begins and results in inconsistency.

There is a major problem facing the Hebrew Christian concerning the Law of Moses, and the solution lies in discovering what the Bible says about the Hebrew Christian's relationship to the Law, especially the Ten Commandments.

THE UNITY OF THE LAW OF MOSES

To begin with, it must be understood that the Mosaic Law is viewed by the Scriptures as a unit. The word *Torah*, "Law," when applied to the Law of Moses is always singular, although it contains 613 commandments. The same is true of the Greek word *Nomos* in the New Testament. The division of the Law of Moses into ceremonial, legal, and moral parts is convenient for the study of the different types of commandments contained within it, but it is never divided in this way by the Scriptures themselves. Neither is there any scriptural basis for separating the Ten Commandments from the whole 613 and making only the Ten perpetual. All 613 commandments are a single unit comprising the Law of Moses.

It is the principle of the unity of the Law of Moses that lies behind the statement found in James 2:10:

> For whosoever shall keep the whole law, and yet stumble in one point, he is become guilty of all.

The point is clear. A person needs only to break one of the 613 commandments to be guilty of breaking all of the Law of Moses. This can only be true if the Mosaic Law is a unit. If it is not, the guilt lies only in the particular commandment violated and not in the whole Law. In other words, if one breaks a legal commandment, he is guilty of breaking the ceremonial and moral ones as well. The same is true of breaking a moral or ceremonial commandment. To bring the point closer to home, if a person eats ham, according to the Law of Moses he is guilty of breaking the Ten Commandments, although none of them says anything about ham. The Law is a unit, and to break one of the 613 commandments is to break them all.

In order to have a clear understanding of the Law of Moses and its relationship to the believer, it is necessary to view it as the Scriptures view it: as a unit that cannot be divided into parts that have been done away with and parts that have not.

Nor can certain commandments be separated in such a way as to give them a different status from other commandments.

The Law of Moses has been Rendered Inoperative

The clear-cut teaching of the New Testament is that the Law of Moses has been rendered inoperative with the death of Christ; in other words, the Law in its totality no longer has authority over any individual. This is evident first of all from Romans 10:4:

> For Christ is the end of the law unto righteousness to every one that believeth.

Very clearly, Christ is the end of the Law, and that includes all 613 commandments; hence the Law has ceased to function. There is no justification through it:

> Yet knowing that a man is not justified by the works of the law but through faith in Jesus Christ, even we believed on Christ Jesus, that we might be justified by faith in Christ, and not by the works of the law: because by the works of the law shall no flesh be justified. (Galatians 2:16)

Furthermore, there is no sanctification or perfection through the Law:

> (For the law made nothing perfect), and a bringing in thereupon of a better hope, through which we draw nigh unto God. (Hebrews 7:19)

Thus it should be very evident that the Law has come to an end in Christ and cannot function in justification or sanctification. For the believer especially it has been rendered inoperative; the remaining verses, however, show that the Law has ceased to function for all.

Secondly, the Law was never meant to be a permanent administration but rather a temporary one:

> What then is the law? It was added because of transgressions, till the seed should come to whom the promise hath been made.... (Galatians 3:19)

In the context, Paul is pointing to the Law of Moses as an addition to the Abrahamic Covenant. It was added for the purpose of making sin very clear so that all will know that they have fallen short of God's standard for righteousness. It was a temporary addition until the seed (Christ) would come; now that he has come, the Law is finished. The addition has ceased to function with the cross.

Thirdly, with Christ there is a new priesthood according to the order of Melchizedek, not according to the order of Aaron. The Law of Moses provided the basis for the Levitical Priesthood. Thus a new priesthood required a new law under which it could operate. This is clear from Hebrews 7:11-12, 18:

> Now if there was perfection through the Levitical priesthood (for under it hath the people received the law), what further need was there that another priest should arise after the order of Melchizedek, and not be reckoned after the order of Aaron? For the priesthood being changed, there is made of necessity a change also of the law.... For there is a disannulling of a foregoing commandment because of its weakness and unprofitableness.

Consequently, the Law of Moses has been disannulled in favor of a new law, which is the basis for the priesthood according to the order of Melchizedek.

The fourth line of evidence for the annulment of the Mosaic Law zeros right in on that part of the Law that most people want to retain, the Ten Commandments:

> Ye are our epistle, written in our hearts, known and read of all men; being made manifest that ye are an epistle of Christ,

ministered by us, written not with ink, but with the Spirit of
the living God; not in tables of stone, but in tables that are
hearts of flesh. And such confidence have we through Christ
to God-ward: not that we are sufficient of ourselves, to account
anything as from ourselves; but our sufficiency is from God;
who also made us sufficient as ministers of a new covenant;
not of the letter, but of the spirit: for the letter killeth, but
the spirit giveth life. But if the ministration of death, written,
and engraven on stones, came with glory, so that the children
of Israel could not look stedfastly upon the face of Moses for
the glory of his face; which glory was passing away: how
shall not rather the ministration of the spirit be with glory?
For if the ministration of condemnation hath glory, much
rather doth the ministration of righteousness exceed in glory.
For verily that which hath been made glorious hath not been
made glorious in this respect, by reason of the glory that sur-
passeth. For if that which passeth away was with glory, much
more that which remaineth is in glory. (II Corinthians 3:2-11)

First of all, one needs to see what Paul is saying concerning
the Law of Moses. In verse seven it is called the *ministration of
death*. In verse nine it is called the *ministration of condemnation*. These are negative but valid descriptions. In verses three
and seven the spotlight is on the Ten Commandments since it
is these which were *engraven on stones*. The main point then is
that the Law of Moses, especially as represented by the Ten
Commandments, is a ministration of death and a ministration
of condemnation. If the Ten Commandments were still in force
today, this would still be true.

But they are no longer in force, for it states in verses seven
and eleven that the Law has passed away. The Greek word used
is *katargeo*, which means "to render inoperative." Since the
emphasis in this passage is on the Ten Commandments, this
means that the Ten Commandments have passed away. The
thrust is very clear. The Law of Moses, and especially the Ten
Commandments, is no longer in effect. In fact, the superiority
of the Law of Christ is seen by the fact that it will never be rendered inoperative (verses 9-11).

To summarize, the Law is a unit comprised of 613 commandments, and all of it has been invalidated. There is no commandment that has continued beyond the cross of Christ. The Law is there and can be used as a teaching tool to show God's standard of righteousness and man's sinfulness and need of a substitutionary atonement. It can be used to point one to Christ (Galatians 3:23-25). However, it has completely ceased to function as an authority over individuals.

THE HEBREW CHRISTIAN IS UNDER A NEW LAW

The Law of Moses has been disannulled and we are now under a new law. This new law is called the Law of Christ in Galatians 6:2 and the Law of the Spirit of Life in Romans 8:2. This is a brand new law totally separate from the Law of Moses.

The reason why there is so much confusion here is that the Law of Christ contains many commandments similar to those found in the Mosaic Law, and many have concluded that certain sections of the Law have therefore been retained. But it has already been shown that this cannot be the case, and the explanation for the sameness of the commandments is to be found elsewhere.

The explanation can best be understood if it is realized that there are a number of codes in the Bible, such as the Edenic, Adamic, Noahic, Mosaic, and Christian. A new code will always contain some of the same commandments of the previous code, but this does not mean that the previous code is still in effect. While certain of the commandments of the Adamic Code were also found in the Edenic Code, it did not mean that the Edenic Code was still partially in force; it ceased to function with the fall of man. The same is true when we compare the Law of Christ with the Law of Moses. There are many similar commandments. For example, nine of the Ten Commandments are to be found in the Law of Christ. But this does not mean that the Law of Moses is still in force.

Let me illustrate by using an example which many of us have experienced. I received my first driver's license in the state of California, and as long as I drove in California I was subject to the traffic laws of that state. But after a couple of years I moved to New York. Once I left California, I ceased to be under California traffic law. The traffic laws of that state were rendered inoperative in my case. Now my driving was subject to a new law, the traffic laws of the state of New York. There were many laws which were different. In California I was permitted to make a right turn at a red light after stopping and yielding the right-of-way. But in New York no turn was permitted at a red light. There were many similar laws between the two states, such as the law demanding that I stop at a red light. But when I stopped at a red light, I did not do so in obedience to the state of California, as I once had, but in obedience to the state of New York. I proceeded at a green light not because of California law but because of New York law. If I went through a red light without stopping, I was not guilty of breaking California law but New York law. Many laws were similar, but they were under two distinctly different systems.

The law of Moses has been nullified, and we are now under the Law of Christ. There are many different commandments; under the Law of Moses we would not be permitted to eat pork, but under the Law of Christ we may. There are many similar commandments, but they are nonetheless in two separate systems. So if we do not kill or steal, this is not because of the Law of Moses but because of the Law of Christ. On the other hand, if I steal, I am not guilty of breaking the Law of Moses but of breaking the Law of Christ.

This understanding can solve many problems among fundamental believers, such as the issues of women wearing pants, the Sabbath, and tithing. If the commandments concerning these things are only based on the Law of Moses and not on the Law of Christ, then they have no validity for the New Testament believer. This brings up the issue of legalism, but comment on this will be reserved for a later chapter.

THE PRINCIPLE OF FREEDOM

As we have been saying, the believer in Christ is free from the Law of Moses. This means that he is free from the necessity of keeping any commandment of that system. But on the other hand, he is also free to keep parts of the Law of Moses if he so desires.

The biblical basis for this freedom to keep the Law can be seen in the actions of Paul, the greatest exponent of freedom from the Law. His vow in Acts 18:18 is based on Numbers 6:2, 5, 9, and 18. His desire to be in Jerusalem for Pentecost in Acts 20:16 is based on Deuteronomy 16:16. The strongest passage is Acts 21:17-26, where we see Paul, the apostle of freedom from the Law, himself keeping the Law:

> And when we were come to Jerusalem, the brethren received us gladly. And the day following Paul went in with us unto James; and all the elders were present. And when he had saluted them, he rehearsed one by one the things which God had wrought among the Gentiles through his ministry. And they, when they heard it, glorified God; and they said unto him, Thou seest, brother, how many thousands there are among the Jews of them that have believed; and they are all zealous for the law: and they have been informed concerning thee, that thou teachest all the Jews who are among the Gentiles to forsake Moses, telling them not to circumcise their children neither to walk after the customs. What is it therefore? they will certainly hear that thou art come. Do therefore this that we say to thee: We have four men that have a vow on them; these take, and purify thyself with them, and be at charges for them, that they may shave their heads: and all shall know that there is no truth in the things whereof they have been informed concerning thee; but that *thou thyself also walkest orderly, keeping the law*. But as touching the Gentiles that have believed, we wrote, giving judgment that they should keep themselves from things sacrificed to idols, and from blood, and from what is strangled, and from fornication. Then Paul took the men, and the next day purifying himself

with them went into the temple, declaring the fulfillment of the days of purification, until the offering was offered for every one of them. (Italics supplied)

The believer is free from the Law, but he is also free to keep parts of it. Thus if a Hebrew Christian feels the need to refrain from eating pork, he is free to do so. The same is true for all the other commandments.

However, there are two dangers that must be avoided by the Hebrew Christian who volunteers to keep commandments of the Law of Moses. One danger is the idea that by doing so he is contributing to his own justification and sanctification. This is false and should be avoided. The second danger is in one's expecting others to keep the same commandments he has decided to keep. This is equally wrong and borders on legalism. The one who exercises his freedom to keep the Law must recognize and respect another's freedom not to keep it.

CHAPTER VII

HEBREW CHRISTIANITY AND THE
LOCAL CHURCH

When a Jew first becomes a believer and joins the ranks of
Hebrew Christians, he faces two practical problems: baptism
and church membership. Any reluctance to be baptized is because of two reasons. First, baptism in his mind is something so
Gentile that to submit to it is to become a non-Jew; secondly, it
marks the point of separation from Judaism, the synagogue, and
the Jewish community. The first difficulty is soon resolved as
the new believer studies the Scriptures, sees the true meaning
of baptism, and follows the command of Christ.

The problem of church membership is not so easily solved.
The factors are more numerous and more complicated than
those involved in baptism. To get a proper perspective, we will
approach this question by looking at the exact nature of the
issues and then at the biblical and practical solutions as over
against the non-biblical ones.

The Problems of Hebrew Christians
in Relation to the Local Church

On the Side of the Local Church

First of all, the local church today is a Gentile-cultured church
and is quite foreign to most Jews. It is a culture from which a
Jew shies away, not because he feels that the Jewish culture is
superior, but simply because the Gentile culture is strange.
Such things as crosses, legalistic do's and don'ts, and church

procedures are very Gentile. These do not come out of the Scriptures but have developed in the course of history with Gentile domination of the church. This does not mean that influence of Gentile culture is biblically wrong. It simply means that it is not Jewish.

Anti-Semitism is a second problem in many local churches. Those with a more aggressive anti-Semitism will not allow a Hebrew Christian to join. A less aggressive congregation will extend him membership but will not make him feel welcome, demanding that he give up everything Jewish. One Hebrew Christian couple to whom I have ministered came to know their Messiah through the reading of the New Testament. Not having any Christian friends or counseling or any understanding of the different types of churches, they joined a nearby congregation, which in this case happened to be Lutheran. They were allowed to become members but then were taught they were no longer Jews and therefore had to give up everything Jewish. They were told to stop speaking Yiddish, to stop eating Jewish foods, to refrain from going to Jewish restaurants, and to forget all that was in any way related to their Jewishness. They followed these instructions for about a year living in constant fear. If a Yiddish phrase slipped through their tongues or they had a yearning for a bagel, they would feel guilty. The strain proved too much for them and they left the church. It was years before they were ready to attend a local church again. Similar incidents continue to occur to a greater or lesser degree in many local churches and present a definite problem to the Hebrew Christian.

A third difficulty concerning the local church is insensitivity to the needs of the Hebrew Christian. A Hebrew Christian, by virtue of his position, faces certain identity problems that the Gentile Christian never has. The local church is often well-equipped to handle the problems of Gentile Christians but not those of Jewish Christians. This insensitivity is the result of ignorance and misunderstanding rather than of deliberate neglect. It is unfortunate that Gentile Christians acquainted with the problems of former alcoholics and dope addicts who have become believers do not realize that the problems of the new Hebrew Christian are equally great. This indifference has driven many Hebrew Christians out of local congregations.

Pro-Semitism, a good thing in itself, is sometimes a fourth problem. Often a Hebrew Christian is so fussed over that it appears God must expend more energy and grace to save a Jew than a Gentile. Some Hebrew Christians revel in all this attention and really eat it up. But for others it is strange and unnatural and makes them shy away from the local church.

On the Side of the Hebrew Christian

One major difficulty for the Hebrew Christian is the fear of losing his Jewish identity. Coming into a local church dominated by Gentile Christians and Gentile culture poses a threat to that identity. Since his own culture is rich with heritage and history, he naturally does not wish to lose it. If he does not fear for himself, he will often fear for his children, who are not likely to get any Jewish culture or history in the church Sunday School. To drown his Jewishness in the sea of Gentile culture is something the Hebrew Christian does not want to happen, and often this is used as an excuse not to join the local church.

A second problem is legalism. Fundamentalists, especially in the United States, have developed extensive laws making activities such as dancing, drinking of wine, and seeing movies into sin. Although this is often clearly not biblical, they have become so engraved into the local church as to make them equally inspired with the Ten Commandments and the Sermon on the Mount. A Hebrew Christian, who more than anyone else has been freed from the Law, finds this new system of law more of a burden than that of Moses. To make sins of wine and dancing, both strong elements in the Jewish culture, and then to tell the Hebrew Christian that he must give them up, will often turn

him away. Since the Bible does not condemn these things whereas the local church does, this inconsistency causes the Hebrew
Christian to avoid the local church.

A third problem is the Hebrew Christian's desire to continue
practicing certain celebrations of Judaism, such as the Passover,
and to give his children a Jewish education. These are not possible in the local church, and so often this too becomes a barrier to
the Jewish believer's uniting with it.

The Non-Biblical Solutions

Separation from the Local Church

Because of these problems, two extreme solutions have been
used. The first extreme is separation from the Christian community altogether. The individual Jewish believer does not
join a local church, does not attend Christian functions except
on rare occasions, and avoids having Gentile Christian friends.
He attends meetings of Hebrew Christians and has Hebrew
Christian friends but otherwise has little contact with other
believers.

While this extreme does succeed in avoiding contact with
Gentile culture, this is not the biblical solution. It does not give
the Hebrew Christian the opportunity of using his spiritual
gifts for the building up of the local body, and it is in direct disobedience to a command written particularly to Hebrew Christians:

> Not forsaking our own assembling together, as the custom of
> some is, but exhorting one another; and so much the more, as
> ye see the day drawing nigh. (Hebrews 10:25)

The Hebrew Christian Church

The second extreme is the formation of the local Hebrew
Christian church. Gentile membership and participation is often
limited to those who are married to Hebrew Christians or are

involved in Hebrew Christian work. This method also succeeds in avoiding Gentile Christian culture and in achieving the up-bringing of children as Jews as well as believers.

But this solution raises some problems of its own. For instance, on what biblical basis can Gentiles be excluded from or limited in membership in the local church? There is no biblical basis for excluding a Gentile believer from membership because he is Gentile. Yet if a Hebrew Christian church has open membership, and if the Gentile Christians again outnumber the Hebrew Christians, then the problem that the Hebrew Christian church was founded to solve develops again.

The main problem with a Hebrew Christian church, how-ever, is that it goes against the biblical ideal of Gentile and Jewish believers worshipping and functioning together in the local church. Separation from Gentile believers is denounced in Galatians 2:11-13:

> But when Cephas came to Antioch, I resisted him to the face, because he stood condemned. For before that certain came from James, he ate with the Gentiles; but when they came, he drew back and separated himself, fearing them that were of the circumcision. And the rest of the Jews dissembled likewise with him; insomuch that even Barnabas was carried away with their dissimulation.

Establishing Hebrew Christian churches is not the solution to the problem. By and large the attempts have been few and not very successful. Even Hebrew Christian churches in cities have not been able to attract most Hebrew Christians of those cities. Besides, such a solution robs the local church of the benefits it can derive from having Hebrew Christian members.

A Biblical Solution

The Local Church

The biblical pattern for the local church is pictured in Ephe-sians 2:11-22:

Wherefore remember, that once ye, the Gentiles in the flesh, who are called Uncircumcision by that which is called Circumcision, in the flesh, made by hands; that ye were at that time separate from Christ, alienated from the commonwealth of Israel, and strangers from the covenants of the promise, having no hope and without God in the world. But now in Christ Jesus ye that once were far off are made nigh in the blood of Christ. For he is our peace, who made both one, and brake down the middle wall of partition, having abolished in his flesh the enmity, even the law of commandments contained in ordinances; that he might create in himself of the two one new man, so making peace; and might reconcile them both in one body unto God through the cross, having slain the enmity thereby: and he came and preached peace to you that were far off, and peace to them that were nigh: for through him we both have our access in one Spirit unto the Father. So then ye are no more strangers and sojourners, but ye are fellow-citizens with the saints, and of the household of God, being built upon the foundation of the apostles and prophets, Christ Jesus himself being the chief corner stone; in whom each several building, fitly framed together, groweth into a holy temple in the Lord; in whom ye also are builded together for a habitation of God in the Spirit.

Granted, Paul is mainly talking about the invisible church; but the point is that the pattern for the visible church should be one of Jews and Gentiles forming one Body in Christ. The visible church is comprised of a body of professing and baptized believers united for the purpose of worship, practice of the ordinances, and carrying out of the Great Commission. This body of believers is to contain both Jews and Gentiles.

If this had been the pattern followed by the church throughout the centuries, it could have saved itself a great amount of doctrinal error. For no Jew would have remained in the local church and allowed anyone to challenge the authority of the Scriptures or to deny the Virgin Birth and the Resurrection. The church has lost much in failing to bring the gospel to the Jew. Charles H. Stevens clearly portrays this fact in a booklet titled *What It Has Cost the Church to Withold Christ from the Jews.* *

There are some practical benefits from the Hebrew Christian's joining the local church. The most important is his ability to contribute to the growth of the church through the use of his spiritual gifts. The second is his ability to educate the Gentile believers in their obligation to the Jew and Jewish missions. Thirdly, there are many passages of Scripture which are peculiarly Jewish and which only a person with a Jewish background would be able to explain, such as the two cups mentioned in Luke 22:14-20 in connection with the Passover. His very presence is a witness to the Jewishness of the Christian faith, of the Scriptures, and of the Saviour.

The Jew in the church can be the discerner between the teaching and mores in the church that are truly scriptural and those that are not. He can be the one to distinguish between what is biblical and what is really a product of Gentile culture.

The Jew can stem the tide of anti-Semitism by teaching what God feels about one's attitude to the Jews and by teaching the church how to receive the Hebrew Christian and be sensitive to his problems as a new believer.

Thus the teaching of Scripture would be against both total separation from the local church and separation by forming strictly Hebrew Christian congregations. The local church must be composed where possible of both Jewish and Gentile believers working together for the cause of Christ. It is to the praise of most Hebrew Christians that they have chosen to follow this course and not the two extremes.

The Hebrew Christian Fellowship

But what about the problem of retaining Jewish identity? Of raising children in the Jewish culture? Of practicing Jewish festivals? As has been shown, it is not biblical to form a local church composed only of Hebrew Christians. But having joined

*Available through the American Board of Missions to the Jews.

a local church, the Hebrew Christian cannot expect it to help him in retaining his Jewish identity. This is not the function of the local church. Although the local congregation today is Gentile-cultured, the Hebrew Christian cannot expect this centuries-old culture to be suddenly dropped for his benefit any more than the Gentile Christian has a right to expect the Hebrew Christian to drop his Jewishness.

The solution is not to organize separate Hebrew Christian churches, thus violating the biblical norm, but to organize Hebrew Christian Fellowships where believing Jews can come together as often as they like. Such a fellowship would help to meet the needs of new believers, hold children's classes in Jewish studies, become a center for Jews to reach out to unbelieving Jews, and be a place where Hebrew Christians can gather to study the Scriptures in a Jewish context and perform the functions involved in the various Jewish celebrations.

The American Board of Missions to the Jews has taken the lead in this area through their Beth Sar Shalom Hebrew Christian Fellowships in major cities around the country. These fellowships function both as evangelistic mission branches of the ABMJ and as centers where Hebrew Christians can come together.

Such a fellowship, however, must have some guidelines by which to function. It must never be viewed as, or take the role of, a substitute for the local church. Hebrew Christian members must be encouraged to take their rightful place in the local church and participate in its functions as well. Furthermore, the meetings planned at the fellowship must not be held at the same time as major church functions, i.e., the Sunday morning and evening services and, in many cases in the United States, the Wednesday night services.

The Hebrew Christian Fellowship must never become an end in itself, but it should be a place where the Jewish unbeliever can be brought and yet feel somewhat at home, although the center of the message is still Jesus Christ.

The leader of a Hebrew Christian Fellowship does not necessarily have to be Jewish himself. But a Gentile leader, to be effective, must be acculturated to be able to identify realistically with the Jewish people. Unfortunately, there are Gentile leaders of Hebrew Christian Fellowships who have either refused or made no real attempt towards acculturation, and so often they are simply playing a role. Their meetings are often a game called "Let's Play Jewish." Understandably in such a case, most of the people in attendance are Gentiles who wish to play the same game. To throw out a few Jewish words or phrases does not really mean one is acculturated. On the other hand, other Gentiles have acculturated so beautifully that often many of the Jews who come do not realize that they are not Jewish.

The Hebrew Christian Fellowship can be a place where the festivals of Israel and evangelistic or worship services of special Jewish character can be conducted. But all services must be in accordance and consistent with our faith in Christ. More will be said on this point later.

CONCLUSION

The Hebrew Christian should be a member of the local church along with Gentile believers. Most Hebrew Christians have taken this course. But the Jewish culture and identity can be retained through the Hebrew Christian Fellowship. Whether it is in the form of a Jewish mission, such as the Beth Sar Shalom Hebrew Christian Fellowships of the American Board of Missions to the Jews, or of branches of the Hebrew Christian Alliance, is not the issue; both certainly have equal value. The Hebrew Christian distinctive has already been shown to exist through the Abrahamic Covenant, and the identity needs to be retained. This is a way to do it.

CHAPTER VIII

MISSIONS

One of the functions of the local assembly is to carry out the Great Commission of Matthew 28:18-20:

> And Jesus came to them and spake unto them, saying, All authority hath been given unto me in heaven and on earth. Go ye therefore, and make disciples of all the nations, baptizing them into the name of the Father and of the Son and of the Holy Spirit: teaching them to observe all things whatsoever I commanded you: and lo, I am with you always, even unto the end of the world.

Hebrew as well as Gentile Christianity has recognized the need for world-wide evangelism in fulfilling the Great Commission and has contributed to it heavily both in man power and financial support. But Hebrew Christianity has recognized an aspect of the biblical method that the major part of Gentile Christianity has either ignored, denied or rebelled against. Although the Scriptures are rather clear on the point of proper methodology, it is one that creates a negative reaction sometimes bordering on anti-Semitism. Other times it is obvious that anti-Semitism is the source of the reaction. The methodology is a matter of procedure, and the procedure is depicted in Romans 1:16:

> For I am not ashamed of the gospel: for it is the power of God unto salvation to every one that believeth; to the Jew first, and also to the Greek.

The gospel is the power of God, and the proper procedure

is for it to go to the Jew first. The governing verb is in the present tense for both clauses: the gospel *is* the power of God and the gospel *is* to the Jew first. To interpret this verse historically to mean the gospel *was* to the Jew first in the sense that it came to him first and this is no longer the case, or that it was only true during the apostolic period, is also to say that the gospel *was* the power of God and that it is no longer. Consistent exegesis would demand that if the gospel is always the power of God, then it is always to the Jew first.

Applying this verse to the Great Commission, the gospel, wherever and by whatever means it goes out from the local church, must go to the Jew first. This is the biblical procedure for evangelism regardless of the method (radio, street meetings, literature, door-to-door, mass evangelism, etc.). Since most believers and local assemblies participate in the Great Commission mainly through monetary giving, this would require giving to the Jew first. This is true of the individual believer as well as of the local assembly in their missionary budget.

What is true of the local church is also true of the missionary in the field. He must first take the gospel to any Jews who may be in the field where he is working. Regardless of his particular place of calling, his obligation is to seek out the Jews and present them with the gospel. Where there is already a command, no special leading is necessary.

Many missionaries may object, but fortunately we have a biblical and an apostolic example in Paul, although he was not called to the Jews.

> But I speak to you that are Gentiles. Inasmuch then as I am an apostle of Gentiles, I glorify my ministry; if by any means I may provoke to jealousy them that are my flesh, and may save some of them. (Romans 11:13-14)

On this point his ministry was different from Peter's:

> But contrariwise, when they saw that I had been intrusted

with the gospel of the uncircumcision, even as Peter with the gospel of the circumcision (for he that wrought for Peter unto the apostleship of the circumcision wrought for me also unto the Gentiles); and when they perceived the grace that was given unto me, James and Cephas and John, they who were reputed to be pillars, gave to me and Barnabas the right hands of fellowship, that we should go unto the Gentiles, and they unto the circumcision. (Galatians 2:7-9)

Even though Paul's unique calling and ministry was to the Gentiles, the great apostle recognized the principle of Romans 1:16 and went to the Jew first wherever he visited. To substantiate this fact, we will follow the footsteps of the apostle in the book of Acts.

The beginning of his mission to the Gentiles is found in Acts 13:2-3:

And as they ministered to the Lord, and fasted, the Holy Spirit said, Separate me Barnabas and Saul for the work whereunto I have called them. Then, when they had fasted and prayed and laid their hands on them, they sent them away.

But Paul proceeds to the Jew first.

So they, being sent forth by the Holy Spirit, went down to Seleucia; and from thence they sailed to Cyprus. And when they were at Salamis, they proclaimed the word of God in the synagogues of the Jews: and they had also John as their attendant. (13:4-5)

But they, passing through from Perga, came to Antioch of Pisidia; and they went into the synagogue on the sabbath day, and sat down. (13:14)

And it came to pass in Iconium that they entered together into the synagogue of the Jews, and so spake that a great multitude both of Jews and of Greeks believed. (14:1)

Setting sail therefore from Troas, we made a straight course to Samothrace, and the day following to Neapolis; and from thence to Philippi, which is a city of Macedonia, the first of the district, a Roman colony: and we were in this city tarrying certain days. And on the sabbath day we went forth without the gate by a river side, where we supposed there was a place of prayer; and we sat down, and spake unto the women that were come together. (16:11-13) (Since this was a Sabbath prayer meeting, this group was obviously Jewish.)

Now when they had passed through Amphipolis and Apollonia, they came to Thessalonica, where was a synagogue of the Jews: and Paul, *as his custom was,* went in unto them, and for three sabbath days reasoned with them from the scriptures. (17:1-2) (Italics added)

And the brethren immediately sent away Paul and Silas by night unto Berea: who when they were come thither went into the synagogue of the Jews. (17:10)

Now while Paul waited for them at Athens, his spirit was provoked within him as he beheld the city full of idols. So he reasoned in the synagogue with the Jews and the devout persons, and in the marketplace every day with them that met him. (17:16-17)

The preceding passage is one of the clearest examples of Paul's procedure in presenting the gospel. First of all, he is disturbed over the mass idolatry in Athens and desires to preach to the Gentile idol worshippers. (No Jews were worshipping these idols; idolatry was not a problem in this stage of Jewish history.) But although he wants to preach to the idol worshippers, he knows what God's procedure is. So in verse seventeen he presents the claims of Christ to the Jews, and then in verse eighteen he finally goes to the Gentiles.

After these things he departed from Athens, and came to Corinth. And he found a certain Jew named Aquila, a man of Pontus by race, lately come from Italy, with his wife Priscilla, because Claudius had commanded all the Jews to depart from Rome: and he came unto them; and because he was of the same trade, he abode with them, and they wrought; for by their trade they were tentmakers. And he reasoned in the synagogue every sabbath, and persuaded Jews and Greeks. (18:1-4)

And they came to Ephesus, and he left them there: but he himself entered into the synagogue, and reasoned with the Jews. (18:19)

And it came to pass, that, while Apollos was at Corinth, Paul having passed through the upper country came to Ephesus, and found certain disciples. . . . And he entered into the synagogue, and spake boldly for the space of three months, reasoning and persuading as to the things concerning the kingdom of God. (19:1,8)

And when we entered into Rome, Paul was suffered to abide by himself with the soldier that guarded him. And it came to pass, that after three days he called together those that were the chief of the Jews. . . . (28:16-17)

Right to the very end of the book of Acts, Paul is presenting the gospel to the Jews first. Even after returning to a city where he had already established a church, he first went to the Jews.

Although the Scriptures are very clear about this procedure, it is nevertheless denied by many. A major argument used to refute this doctrine is based on Acts 28:25-28:

And when they agreed not among themselves, they departed after that Paul had spoken one word, Well spake the Holy Spirit through Isaiah the prophet unto your fathers, saying, Go thou unto this people, and say, By hearing ye shall hear, and shall in no wise understand; And seeing ye shall see, and shall in no wise perceive: For this people's heart is waxed gross, And their ears are full of hearing, And their eyes they have closed; Lest haply they should perceive with their eyes, And hear with their ears, And understand with their heart, And should turn again, And I should heal them. Be it known therefore unto you, that this salvation of God is sent unto the Gentiles: they will also hear.

Because of these concluding words and Paul's declaration that the gospel will now go to the Gentiles, the passage is taken to mean that the gospel is no longer to the Jew first and that God has now changed his program of evangelism, superseding Romans 1:16.

It is agreed that Romans was written before Acts, but this passage does not mean that the gospel is no longer to the Jew first or that God has changed his program of evangelism. The true meaning is to be found in comparison with two other passages where these words had been spoken before:

> And the next sabbath almost the whole city was gathered together to hear the word of God. But when the Jews saw the multitudes, they were filled with jealousy, and contradicted the things which were spoken by Paul, and blasphemed. And Paul and Barnabas spake out boldly, and said, It was necessary that the word of God should first be spoken to you. Seeing ye thrust it from you, and judge yourselves unworthy of eternal life, lo, we turn to the Gentiles. For so hath the Lord commanded us, saying, I have set thee for a light of the Gentiles, That thou shouldest be for salvation unto the uttermost part of the earth. And as the Gentiles heard this, they were glad, and glorified the word of God: and as many as were ordained to eternal life believed. (Acts 13:44-48)

> But when Silas and Timothy came down from Macedonia, Paul was constrained by the word, testifying to the Jews that Jesus was the Christ. And when they opposed themselves and blasphemed, he shook out his raiment and said unto them, Your blood be upon your own heads; I am clean: from henceforth I will go unto the Gentiles. (Acts 18:5-6)

The true interpretation of Acts 28:25-28 is to be seen in these two passages, which indicate a local change and not an overall change in the program of evangelism. In the first passage, the Jews of Antioch of Pisidia rejected the gospel; so now in Antioch of Pisidia Paul will go to the Gentiles. In the second passage the Jews of Corinth rejected the gospel; so now Paul will turn to the Gentiles of Corinth. But when he left both Antioch of Pisidia and Corinth for new territory, he went back to the Jew first. Furthermore, when he returned to Corinth in chapter nineteen, he again went to the Jew first, even after his declaration in the previous chapter of going to the Gentiles.

What was true of Antioch of Pisidia and Corinth is also true of Rome. The Jews of Rome had rejected the gospel, and now Paul will go to the Gentiles of Rome. There is no shift in the procedure of presenting the gospel. Acts 28 is only a continuation of the procedure already in progress of presenting the gospel to the Jew first and then turning to the Gentiles. If Paul left Rome after two years (and I believe that he did), he again repeated after Rome what he repeated after Antioch of Pisidia and Corinth; he went to the Jew first.

Thus the position of Hebrew Christianity in relation to missions is that the gospel must be to the Jew first. This is not a matter of preference but a matter of procedure. It is in the outworking of the Abrahamic Covenant in this area that the local congregation can appropriate certain blessings, for in giving the gospel to the Jew first the church is blessing the Jews. There are certain blessings which the local church will always have as long as the gospel is preached from the pulpit and the local assembly stands true to the fundamentals of the faith. But there are some blessings which are based on other conditions. Thus the blessings of the Abrahamic Covenant available to the local congregation are conditioned upon the congregation's blessing the Jews, by presenting the gospel to the Jew first. So if the Jews in the neighborhood of the local church are not being evangelized, attempts by the church to reach them ought to be made. If the missionaries of the church are not reaching out to the Jewish community in their field of service, they ought to be encouraged to do so. If there is no Jewish mission board on the missionary budget of the church, one should be found and placed there. Then the local church can begin appropriating the blessings of the Abrahamic Covenant, blessings that cannot be obtained any other way.

CHAPTER IX

HEBREW CHRISTIANITY AND JUDAISM

MODERN JUDAISM AND ITS RELATIONSHIP TO HEBREW CHRISTIANITY

Modern Judaism can be defined simply as the religion of many Jews. It is no longer really safe to say most Jews. It has already been demonstrated that Jews themselves cannot be defined on the basis of religion. In the United States there are three different kinds of Judaism which are "recognized" as valid: Orthodox, Conservative, and Reform. Each is subdivided into lesser and greater degrees ranging from the ultra-orthodoxy of Hasidism to atheism in the Reform section. In Israel the division is more simple: a person is either religious or non-religious. This distinction is not based so much on what one believes as it is on degree of practice.

Modern Judaism is not the same as biblical Judaism, nor is it the "father of Christianity." At best it can be called its brother, and biblical Judaism is the father of both. Of the different types of Judaism, Hebrew Christianity has more in common with Orthodox Judaism than with the other two major forms. In fact, there is more common ground between Hebrew Christianity and Orthodox Judaism than between the latter and Reform Judaism.

The purpose of this chapter is not to give an exposition of modern Judaism but rather to show the relationship between it and Hebrew Christianity. There is an abundance of beauty in Judaism, and Hebrew Christians value and appreciate much of it and the part it has played in Jewish history. Nevertheless, we recognize its failure to see Messianic fulfillment in Jesus of

Nazareth. All too often we see it as a religion of externals rather than as a real and personal relationship with God through the Messiah.

Modern Judaism has many practices, rules, and beliefs which are not found in Scripture but have developed in the course of history through Rabbinical and Talmudic traditions. These have equal authority in the eyes of Orthodox Judaism. Since the Bible is the only source of authority to the Hebrew Christian, he rejects these practices as binding and obligatory and is free from any need of observing them. But just as freedom from the Law means freedom also to keep certain aspects of the Law, so freedom from Judaism also frees the Hebrew Christian to keep certain aspects of Judaism, such as the Jewish holy days.

Participation in Jewish Festivals

There are certain advantages for a Hebrew Christian or a Hebrew Christian Fellowship in keeping some or all of the feasts. First, they are good opportunities to share the faith with unbelieving Jewish people, showing how the particular feast points to the Messiahship of Christ.

Secondly, they present a good way of identifying ourselves with the Jewish people. This matter of identification is very important as a testimony to the Jewishness of our faith.

Thirdly, they provide a basis for teaching Jewish culture and history. This is especially important for instilling Jewishness in the children of Hebrew Christians.

Fourthly, they serve as an opportunity to worship God and to thank him for what he has done in the course of Jewish history, and for what he has done for us in the Messiah's fulfillment of the Jewish Holy Days.

However, there is a danger that must be avoided. We cannot celebrate these Holy Days in strict accordance with Judaism. While we are free to copy those things from Judaism which do not go against Scripture, we are not free to use those which do.

Many of the services of Judaism cannot be used in their entirety since there are sections which clearly go against the teaching of the New Testament. The prayer book for Yom Kippur and the Haggadah for Passover are examples of this. While many parts present no real difficulties, there are parts which do. Unfortunately, many Hebrew Christians and some Hebrew Christian Fellowships have not been careful on this point. Often the traditional Orthodox Jewish service has been used and has resulted unknowingly in statements and practices which are quite contrary to what we believe.

The task before us then is to rework many or all of these services in order to bring them into conformity with the teaching of the New Testament concerning our faith in Jesus the Messiah. This cannot be done in the scope of this chapter except to lay down some principles and suggestions for the reworking of these services. Lord willing, the author hopes in the future to be able to rework all of these services and publish them in a separate volume.

Passover. The basic thrust of the Seder on the first night of Passover is to celebrate the redemption from Egypt and retell the story of the Exodus. The Hebrew Christian Haggadah* should retell the story of the Exodus, indicate how Jesus, the Lamb of God, fulfills the Passover, and also bring out the Communion service as Christ did at his Passover. It has become my custom to celebrate the first night of Passover in fellowship with other Jewish believers and then celebrate the second Seder in the privacy of my own home with only a few select friends. I have found this to be very valuable both for me and for the others involved.

Shavuoth. The Feast of Pentecost should be celebrated by reading the Old Testament passages which point to its fulfillment in the birth of the church, the Body of Christ, where Jewish and Gentile believers are united.

*A Hebrew Christian Haggadah has been compiled by the author and is available through the American Board of Missions to the Jews.

Rosh Hashanah. The Feast of Trumpets not only brings in the new year but also prefigures the blowing of trumpets at the rapture and resurrection of the believers. The celebration should include references to that event as well as the reading of Old Testament passages.

Yom Kippur. Unlike Judaism, Hebrew Christianity cannot make the Day of Atonement a day of seeking forgiveness of sins. Instead it should be a memorial day of thanksgiving to God for having forgiven our sins through the death of the Messiah. The readings should include Leviticus 16 and Hebrews 4:14-5:10, 7:1-28, and 9:1-28. The Kol Nidre may also be sung, but the basic thrust of the Hebrew Christian observance must be the atonement through the blood of the Messiah.

Sukkoth. The Hebrew Christian Feast of Tabernacles, as in Judaism, can be celebrated by the building of a booth and the hanging of all the various harvest items. The service can include references to the observance of the feast both in biblical history and during the future Messianic Kingdom, since this feast will be celebrated in the Millennium (Zechariah 14:16-21).

Channukah. The Feast of Lights retells the story of the Maccabees. The Hebrew Christian service can also indicate how Christ, the Light of the World, is a fulfillment of this Feast, and can point to his celebration of it in John 10:22-39.

Purim. The Feast of Lots in the Hebrew Christian celebration should include the reading of the book of Esther in praise of God for the perpetual preservation of the Jewish people on the basis of the Abrahamic Covenant and the believing remnant of Israel.

There are other services which need to be reworked such as a Sabbath service and a Hebrew Christian Wedding service.* All this will take time, but it can be done.

---

*A suggested form for a Hebrew Christian Wedding service will be found in the Appendix.

Hebrew Christians are free to participate in these things, but the guiding principle is that of conformity with our faith in Jesus the Messiah.

GENTILE CHRISTIAN CONVERSION TO JUDAISM

Reasons

In recent years there has been a move among some Gentile Christians to convert to Judaism. There are some who are actively encouraging other Gentile believers to do the same. The reasons are usually based either on one of two doctrinal errors or on a strong desire to identify with the Jewish people.

The first doctrinal error is based on the statement of Christ found in Luke 21:24b:

> . . . Jerusalem shall be trodden down of the Gentiles, until the times of the Gentiles be fulfilled.

Since the Israeli forces captured Jerusalem during the Six Day War, this is supposed to mean the times of the Gentiles have ended and we have now gone back to the times of the Jews. Throughout this present age Jews who became Christians essentially became Gentiles; so now the Gentiles who become Christians are to become Jews.

There are several fallacies involved here. The first is the idea that the times of the Gentiles have ended. The mere fact of Jewish control does not prove this. The Jews have had control of Jerusalem at other periods in their history since the times of the Gentiles began with the Babylonian conquest. The first was during the Maccabean period when the Jews were far more free than they are now to do what they wanted with Jerusalem. During the first revolt against Rome, the Jews exercised full control over Jerusalem for four years, only to lose it again. During the second Jewish revolt under Bar Cochba, the Jews again ex-

ercised full but temporary control. The present Jewish domination is the same as in previous eras during the long period of
the times of the Gentiles. It is temporary. Jerusalem will again
be trodden down by the Gentiles for the last three and a half
years of the Tribulation:

> And there was given me a reed like unto a rod: and one said,
> Rise, and measure the temple of God, and the altar, and them
> that worship therein. And the court which is without the
> temple leave without, and measure it not; for it hath been
> given unto the nations [or Gentiles]: and the holy city shall
> they tread under foot forty and two months. (Revelation
> 11:1-2)

The times of the Gentiles cannot end until Jerusalem can no
longer suffer being dominated by Gentiles. Since there are at
least three and a half more years left in the future for the Gentiles to tread Jerusalem under foot, the times of the Gentiles cannot yet have ended.

Another observation that these adherents fail to make is that
the very part of Jerusalem of which Jesus was speaking is still
virtually all a Gentile city, dominated by its Arab majority.
Furthermore, even a survey study of Daniel 2 and 7 clearly
shows that the times of the Gentiles will end suddenly with the
second coming of Christ. There will be no transitional period.
Gentile domination will be terminated suddenly, quickly, and
permanently with the return of the Messiah.

There is yet another fallacy involved. Jews never become
Gentiles by becoming Christians just because it is the times of
the Gentiles. Nor does returning to the times of the Jews mean
that it is time for Gentiles who are Christians to become Jews.
It is clear from the Scriptures that during the Messianic Age,
when it will really be the times of the Jews, the Jews will still
be Jews and the Gentiles will still be Gentiles. The conclusions
these adherents make just do not follow from their premise.

The second doctrinal error is that by means of converting to

Judaism, the Gentile Christian can become a Jew. That this cannot be has been shown in the first chapter. No rabbi has the power or biblical authority to turn a Gentile into a Jew. For a Gentile believer to whom the Bible is the only ground of authority, it is highly inconsistent to wish to become a Jew on the basis of modern Judaism. No baptism can ever turn a Jew into a Gentile, and no *mikva* can ever turn a Gentile into a Jew.

Biblical Prohibitions

Those Gentile Christians who have converted to Judaism all claim that they never had to renounce their faith in Christ. This may be true, and it is possible to find rabbis who will convert a Gentile to Judaism without requesting that he or she renounce Christ. But this in itself does not solve all the problems. A Gentile, by submitting to conversion to Judaism, is stating, vocally or not, that he accepts the basic tenents of Judaism, one of which is very clear: Jesus is not the Messiah nor has the Messiah yet come. Other tenents are also clearly not biblical. Furthermore, although Christ may not necessarily be renounced, the one who submits to the process of conversion must allow for salvation by another means than by faith in Christ. He is submitting himself to a non-biblical religion.

At best, Gentile Christian converts to Judaism can only call themselves Jews on the basis of modern Jewish law and not on that of Scripture. Yet the very same Jewish law that turns the Gentile into a Jew says that a Jew who believes in Jesus is not a Jew. Thus the Gentile believer who converts to Judaism must hide the fact that he really believes in Jesus. The result is pure dishonesty at conversion and further dishonesty in conduct afterwards.

Finally, is the Gentile Christian desire to become a Jew a biblical one? Not on the basis of I Corinthians 7:18-20:

> Was any man called being circumcised? let him not become uncircumcised. Hath any been called in uncircumcision? let

him not be circumcised. Circumcision is nothing, and uncircumcision is nothing; but the keeping of the commandments of God. Let each man abide in that calling wherein he was called.

As clearly as it can be stated, the command is to remain in the state in which one was when he was saved. If he was saved as a Jew, he is not to seek to become a Gentile. If he was saved as a Gentile, he is not to seek to become a Jew. This passage very clearly forbids a Gentile Christian to convert to Judaism.

The Biblical Pattern

For the Gentile who wants to identify with the Jewish people, we can only say "Amen." But the biblical pattern for doing so is not conversion to Judaism. Another way is specified in I Corinthians 9:19-23:

For though I was free from all men, I brought myself under bondage to all, that I might gain the more. And to the Jews I became as a Jew, that I might gain Jews; to them that are under the law, as under the law, not being myself under the law, that I might gain them that are under the law; to them that are without law, as without law, not being without law to God, but under law to Christ, that I might gain them that are without law. To the weak I became weak, that I might gain the weak: I am become all things to all men, that I may by all means save some. And I do all things for the gospel's sake, that I may be a joint partaker thereof.

The biblical means of identification is by acculturation. To become *as* one is not to become one. This little word is forgotten or ignored by adherents of conversion to Judaism, who use this very same text to prove that their way of identification is by way of conversion. If followed through logically, this would mean that Paul underwent a conversion to become a Gentile when he went to Gentiles, and then reconverted to being a Jew when he again went to Jews, and converted to being weak when he went to the weak, etc. Obviously this is pure nonsense. Identification with the Jews means to become *like* them, to become acculturated. This is the biblical pattern. To convert to Judaism is to violate the Scriptures.

CHAPTER X

THE STATE OF ISRAEL

After centuries of dispersion, persecution, and wanderings, the Jews in 1948 again had a country of their own. Only three years after the collapse of the greatest attempt ever towards the destruction of the Jews, the Jewish state was born and was often run by the very same Jews whom Hitler almost destroyed. A great ingathering has taken place as Jews from all over the world have been immigrating into the Jewish state. Although the vast majority of Jews are still outside the Land, there is nevertheless a nation which all Jews can call home. It is a nation that has survived four wars aimed towards its extinction in a short period of twenty-five years. This dramatic event of history demands and calls for a response from Hebrew Christianity.

It has been stated earlier that the Hebrew Christian is very much involved in the Abrahamic Covenant. He is still a member of the nation descended from Abraham, Isaac, and Jacob, and the promise of the Land as a Jewish possession applies perhaps more to the Hebrew Christian than to anyone else. He has shared the fate of dispersion and persecution along with other Jews, and he now also shares in the blessing of restoration. The state of Israel is his homeland, and his allegiance lies there.

This is not to say that everything Israel does is always right. As a nation, Israel shares the same pitfalls of error and is subject to the same blunders that other nations commit. Israel makes mistakes both in internal and external policies, but no more than other nations. Nevertheless, the Hebrew Christian has a loyalty to the Jewish state that is equal to that of any other Zionist. If

Hebrew Christians have not moved to Israel in the same proportion that other Jews have, it is largely because Hebrew Christians are discriminated against, considered as traitors and non-Jews, and do not have all the equal civil and religious rights as do other Jews. As a result, life becomes hard for them. But these same Hebrew Christians still retain a loyalty to Israel regardless of the negative attitude towards them. In recent years more and more Hebrew Christians have been immigrating to Israel in spite of the hardships, and this is a good sign.

If Hebrew Christians are anything, they are Zionists to the core in a way that non-believing Jews could never be. The most effective fighters of Arab propaganda against Israel in the Christian community have been Hebrew Christians. The results can be seen in what occurred during the days preceding the Six Day War. After years of "Dialogue" with the Jews, liberal Christianity by and large sided with the Arabs, much to the surprise of the Jews. Even more surprising to the Jews was that conservative Christianity, with whom no dialogue existed, came out pro-Israel. This was largely because of the labor of Hebrew Christians found among the ranks of conservative Christianity.

There is another marked difference between the attitude of Hebrew Christians toward Israel and that of other Jews. Because of his understanding of the plan of God, the Hebrew Christian sees the state of Israel in a much greater context. In this context the present state of Israel is only a beginning. It is a dramatic and fantastic beginning, but it is still only a beginning of greater and more fantastic things to come in the outworking of the plan of God in his Messianic Program.

Because the Bible presents the exact details of the Messianic Program, the Hebrew Christian is able to look at world events in relation to Israel, and although he may be concerned, he is not at a loss to understand these events. The War of Independence and the Six Day War, with the Old City falling to Jewish control, all fit nicely into the plan given in the Scriptures. The continual negative attitude towards Israel by that world body of nations, the United Nations, is nothing to be marveled at in the light of biblical prophecy, which states that all nations will come against Jerusalem (Zechariah 12:1-3, 14:1-2). The present-day moves of the Soviet Union into the Middle East against Israel can easily be understood in the context of Ezekiel 38:1-39:16. The Hebrew Christian can look at the state of Israel and still see it as the measure by which God will deal with the Gentile nations. The unbelieving Jewish community can only worry and send funds in hope of Israel's survival. The Hebrew Christian has no fear for the safety of Israel, since He that keeps Israel neither slumbers nor sleeps. (Psalm 121:4)

All of these current events concerning Israel are moving toward the events of the Great Tribulation and will culminate with the second coming of Messiah. Israel will then be established as the head of the nations, and Jerusalem will become the world center and draw all nations to it because God will reign there.

For the Hebrew Christian, the beginning of this goal of the Messianic Program is to be seen in the present state of Israel. He looks upon Israel as one of the great workings of God for the Messianic People. He is loyal to the state of Israel, defends it, and looks forward to greater things to come.

CHAPTER XI

LEGALISM

It is with much hesitation that this chapter is being included in this volume on Hebrew Christianity. In many eyes, this whole work may be discredited because of what is said in this chapter. Yet legalism, especially in the form developed by American fundamentalism,[1] is a product of Gentile Christianity which has become a stumblingblock to many Jewish believers. Many times it has been a problem that has turned the Jewish believer away from the local church.

Legalism, as it is used in this work, is those rules of conduct which are not in the Scriptures but have been developed in the course of church history and have become obligatory upon all Christians if they are to prove themselves true believers. It is not the fact that a believer lives by certain rules or principles not found in the Scriptures which makes him a legalist, but rather his expecting others to follow those same rules.

The number and nature of these extra-biblical rules are different for different parts of the country. Whether it is the Filthy Five, the Nasty Nine, or the Dirty Dozen will depend on the geographical area or on the particular church affiliation of the individual. A person's faith in Christ and his spiritual growth are often judged on the basis of his conformity to these rules rather than on his conformity to the Law of Christ. What is even more unfortunate is that the Law of Christ (those rules specifically found in the New Testament for the believer) and church law (those extra-biblical rules developed by the church) are seldom distinguished, having become one and the same thing.

[1] The author himself is a Fundamentalist.

A Hebrew Christian acquaintance related an incident in the early years of his Christian experience. Entering a church before the start of the service, he began to look around the chapel area. Posted near the door was a list of some twenty things that a true Christian does not do. Few if any were actually found in the Scriptures. The message of the service was along the same lines. During the fellowship time after the service, word got around that he was a Hebrew Christian. At that, one of the leaders came up to him and said, "Aren't you glad that you are out from under the Law?" It was an ironic situation. To him the Hebrew Christian should have been happy to be free from the Law of Moses, and yet he wished to subject the Jewish believer to a whole new law with equal hardships without even the benefit of a biblical basis, which the Law of Moses at least had.

The problem of legalism is a major one to most Hebrew Christians, for they soon realize that this is one of the chief elements that makes the church not so much "Christianized" as "Gentilized," to coin a word. I have met more than one Hebrew Christian who has been driven away from the local church because of this problem. I therefore felt it would be wise to say a few things about this whole area. The things prohibited within legalism are usually referred to as "doubtful things," but to use this expression is to pass judgment on them already. So in this chapter we will refer to them as amoral things.

The Problems of Legalism

Lack of Logic

One of the major problems with legalism is its lack of an objective standard. As a result, many of these rules are based on faulty logic. For example, take the idea that attending movies is wrong. The initial impression seems to be that there is something inherently wrong with movies themselves. But often the same person who feels a Christian should not go to movies finds it perfectly all right to see the same movie on television. So the sin is no longer with the movie itself but rather with the place in which it is seen. So the next question is: why is it wrong to go see that same movie in a theatre? The usual answer is that unbelievers attend or that it is wrong because of what some people do in the back row. But what some people do in the back row is also done in bushes and on benches in the public park. However, a rule against Christians going to a public park is never on the list. The truth of the matter is that most people who go to a movie go to see the movie, just as most people who go to a public park go to enjoy what it has to offer. To condemn a place because of what some people may do there is to condemn all places. It is not logical to pick on movie theatres in particular, for the same reasons apply to many other places.

For a second example, let us take the matter of cards and dice, also found on many lists. Cards are wrong, except maybe for Old Maid or Rook; dice in games like Monopoly are replaced by spinners. To the question of why dice and cards are wrong, the oft-repeated response is that gamblers use them. But murderers, robbers, and gangsters use cars to help them in their work against the law. Applying the same logic, Christians should not drive cars either. But one never hears a sermon on that.

Logic is not an attribute in most rules of legalism. Jews possessing a mind trained in logic find such inconsistency flagrant and appalling.

Confusion as to Where the Sin Lies

A second problem with legalism derives from the first one and can be seen in the same examples. It involves the question of exactly where the sin lies in a particular area. Does the sin lie in the thing itself? Are cards, dice, and movies wrong in themselves, or is the sin in the way they are used? Let us first take a less offensive object: the car. Is the car itself sin, or how that car can be used for sinful purposes? Obviously the latter. Then the same should be true of cards, dice, and movies. If a Christian can drive a car for non-sinful purposes, can he not use cards and dice and go to movies for non-sinful purposes as well? Logically the answer is yes. But because many of the rules of legalism have been so ingrained in us, they are viewed illogically, and there is general confusion over where the sin actually lies.

Faulty Exegesis

A third problem in this area is that the presuppositions of legalism often affect the exegesis of many passages and result in dishonesty. This time we will take the example of wine and use it in a syllogism:

Major Premise: Wine is wrong;
Minor Premise: Jesus would never do anything that is wrong;
— Conclusion: Jesus did not drink wine, but grape juice.

The presupposition used here produces a faulty conclusion because the method of exegesis is faulty. Thus Christ made grape juice in Cana and drank grape juice at the last Passover. Since this faulty presupposition is allowed to stand, it now becomes the judge of Scripture rather than the other way around, and it begins to affect exegesis; wine now means grape juice. The truth of the matter is that both the Hebrew and Greek languages have a perfectly good word for juice, and if that is what the writers of Scripture wanted to say, they could have used it. Instead, they use the Hebrew and Greek words for wine. It just might be that that is exactly what the writers of Scripture through the Holy Spirit intended to say. But rather than letting the Scriptures become the judge of legalism, legalism is allowed to stand with all its presuppositions, and it soon becomes the basis for interpreting the Scriptures.

Antiscriptural

There is a fourth problem which is the most serious. Often certain laws of legalism are clearly non-scriptural. Again let us use the example of wine. In legalism all wine is wrong. But in Psalm 104:15 the writer praises God for creating "wine that maketh glad the heart of man." Drink as much grape juice as you like, it will not have the same effect. But wine does, and God is to be praised for it, according to the Psalmist. But in churches where legalism is the rule of life, no such praise will ever issue from the lips of the believer. Instead, wine itself is condemned rather than the way in which some people use it. The Christian who partakes becomes in their eyes a poor Christian. This attitude is clearly going against Scripture. Wine is part of a Jew's culture, and this antiscriptural outlook becomes a problem for him.

The Law and the Spirit

The fifth problem is that often legalism has a direct effect on an individual's relationship to the Holy Spirit. It is a lot easier for a person to live by a set of rules than to be in such communion with the Holy Spirit as to know what God would want him to do about a certain thing in a given situation. To live by a set rule or list of rules may rob the believer of true communion and of knowing the will of God. It is far superior to live by the Spirit than by the Law. It is harder but greater, for then one depends specifically on the Holy Spirit rather than on a list posted at the church door.

THE BIBLICAL PATTERN

The biblical pattern centers around the Law of Christ. Whatever rules and commandments are specifically stated in the New Testament, the believer is to keep them and requires no special leading for obedience. I do not know if there has ever been a complete list made of all the laws applicable to the New Testament believer as the rabbis have made of the 613 commandments of the Law of Moses. Whether or not there has been, one thing is sure: there are many of them, enough to keep the believer busy for a lifetime. It is to the praise of God's grace that our salvation is not dependent on our ability to keep all these commandments.

Concerning those matters not specifically prohibited in the Scriptures (such as movies, dancing, cards, dice, and wine), these are voluntary and dependent upon individual leading of the Holy Spirit. Just as the one who is free from the Law of Moses is also free to subject himself to certain commands of the Law, so the believer is free to refrain from doing certain things or to subject himself to certain rules, and by doing so he does not become a legalist. But as he begins to insist that others also obey these same rules, he had violated a fellow believer's freedom in Christ and has become a legalist.

BIBLICAL PASSAGES RELATING TO THE PROBLEM OF LEGALISM

Romans 14:1-8

> But him that is weak in faith receive ye, yet not for decision of scruples. One man hath faith to eat all things: but he that is weak eateth herbs. Let not him that eateth set at nought him that eateth not; and let not him that eateth not judge him that eateth: for God hath received him. Who art thou that judgest the servant of another? to his own Lord he standeth or falleth. Yea, he shall be made to stand; for the Lord hath power to make him stand. One man esteemeth one day above another: another esteemeth every day alike. Let each man be fully assured in his own mind. He that regardeth the day, regardeth it unto the Lord: and he that eateth, eateth unto the Lord, for he giveth God thanks; and he that eateth not,

unto the Lord he eateth not, and giveth God thanks. For none of us liveth to himself, and none dieth to himself. For whether we live, we live unto the Lord; or whether we die, we die unto the Lord: whether we live therefore, or die, we are the Lord's.

Several things are brought out in this passage. First of all, it clears up the confusion over who is really the stronger and who is really the weaker believer. In legalism, the ones who are portrayed as the weaker are the ones who practice various things on the forbidden list, while the ones who have abstained are the more spiritual believers. But the very opposite idea is presented in this passage. The believer who has problems with doing certain things and so abstains from doing them is the weaker believer. It is the believer who has the liberty to do these things who is the stronger and more mature.

Secondly, the attitude the two groups are to have towards each other is one of mutual respect. Those who are free to do certain amoral things are not to look down on those who have problems with them. At the same time, those who refrain are not to condemn believers who feel free to participate.

Thirdly, each believer has the right to be persuaded in his own mind concerning amoral issues and then live according to his convictions without expecting others to live in accordance with them.

Fourthly, the principle underlying the doing or not doing of amoral things is our attitude towards God in doing or not doing them. What we give up or what we participate in should be for, and in thanksgiving to God.

Romans 14:14-22

I know, and am persuaded in the Lord Jesus, that nothing is unclean of itself: save that to him who accounteth anything to be unclean, to him it is unclean. For if because of meat thy brother is grieved, thou walkest no longer in love. Destroy not with thy meat him for whom Christ died. Let not then your good be evil spoken of: for the kingdom of God is not eating and drinking, but righteousness and peace and joy in the Holy Spirit. For he that herein serveth Christ is well-pleasing to God, and approved of men. So then let us follow after things which make for peace, and things whereby we may edify one another. Overthrow not for meat's sake the work of God. All things indeed are clean; howbeit it is evil for that man who eateth with offence. It is good not to eat flesh, nor to drink wine, nor to do anything whereby thy brother stumbleth. The faith which thou hast, have thou to thyself before God. Happy is he that judgeth not himself in that which he approveth. But he that doubteth is condemned if he eat, because he eateth not of faith; and whatsoever is not of faith is sin.

More principles can be deduced from this passage. First, nothing is unclean or sin in itself, whether it is a movie, cards, dice, or wine.

Secondly, if a believer considers something to be a sin or unclean, then to him it is sin if he does it; but this does not mean it is sin for another believer to do it.

Thirdly, the person who is free to do or participate in amoral things is to limit his practice by the law of love of the brethren. In other words, how would his doing a given thing in a given situation affect a fellow believer? Different restraints will be required in different situations; no set rule will fit them all. At one point, the free believer may have to refrain from drinking a glass of wine, while at another time there will be no need to refrain. This is biblical situation-ethics, and no rule of total abstention is warranted.

Fourthly, the situation here is not how it will affect an unbeliever or what an unbeliever may think, but rather how it will affect the believer.

Fifthly, the one who is free is happy if he does not judge or condemn himself in doing what he is free to do. But the one who has convictions about doing certain things is sinning when he does them. For whatever is done is to be done in faith. If he has faith to do it, he is to do it without judgment, and if he has faith not to do it, then he is to refrain.

I Corinthians 8:4-13

Concerning therefore the eating of things sacrificed to idols, we know that no idol is anything in the world, and that there is no God but one. For though there be that are called gods, whether in heaven or on earth; as there are gods many, and lords many; yet to us there is one God, the Father, of whom are all things, and we unto him; and one Lord, Jesus Christ, through whom are all things, and we through him. Howbeit there is not in all men that knowledge; but some, being used until now to the idol, eat as of a thing sacrificed to an idol; and their conscience being weak is defiled. But food will not commend us to God: neither, if we eat not, are we the worse; nor, if we eat, are we the better. But take heed lest by any means this liberty of yours become a stumblingblock to the weak. For if a man see thee who hast knowledge sitting at meat in an idol's temple, will not his conscience, if he is weak, be emboldened to eat things sacrificed to idols? For through thy knowledge he that is weak perisheth, the brother for whose sake Christ died. And thus, sinning against the brethren, and wounding their conscience when it is weak, ye sin against Christ. Wherefore, if meat causeth my brother to stumble, I will eat no flesh for evermore, that I cause not my brother to stumble.

We again see the idea that nothing in itself is sin. Meat that is offered to an idol is not bad meat, for the idol is actually nothing. The one who is strong and free is free to eat this meat, although it has been offered to an idol. The character of the meat has not changed regardless of what someone else has done. But a believer who had formerly offered his meat to idols may, in his weakness, feel wrong and have a troubled conscience if he ate it. So for him it would be sin. Putting this into a twentieth century context, a believer is free to drink wine. But another believer, who formerly was an alcoholic or with whom wine was associated with his sinful life, would have a problem with conscience if he partook; so for him it would be sin.

Secondly, those who are free are to be guided again by the effect a certain behavior would have on a brother or a fellow believer. What he may be free to do one day, he may need to refrain from doing on another day. The action must be based on the given situation; there cannot be a cold, hard rule that would cover every circumstance.

Thirdly, the guiding principle in this passage again is not how it would affect an unbeliever but a believer.

Fourthly, the weak believer is the one who has problems with conscience over amoral things, and the strong one is the one who does not have such problems.

I Corinthians 10:23-11:1

All things are lawful; but not all things are expedient. All things are lawful; but not all things edify. Let no man seek his own, but each his neighbor's good. Whatsoever is sold in the shambles, eat, asking no question for conscience' sake; for the earth is the Lord's, and the fulness thereof. If one of them that believe not biddeth you to a feast, and ye are disposed to go; whatsoever is set before you, eat, asking no question for conscience' sake. But if any man say unto you, This hath been offered in sacrifice, eat not, for his sake that showed it, and for conscience's sake: conscience, I say, not thine own, but the other's; for why is my liberty judged by another conscience? If I partake with thankfulness, why am I evil spoken of for that for which I give thanks? Whether therefore ye eat, or drink, or whatsoever ye do, do all to the glory of God. Give no occasion of stumbling, either to Jews, or to Greeks, or to the church of God: even as I also please all men in all things, not seeking mine own profit, but the profit of the many, that they may be saved. Be ye imitators of me, even as I also am of Christ.

Again, nothing is sinful in itself. What is right or wrong is the way in which something is used.

Secondly, the guiding principle is how it affects another person, whether he is a Jew, a Gentile, or a believer. According to this passage we are to be guided by the way an action affects the unbeliever as well as the believer.

Thirdly, what is usually all right may be wrong in a given situation, and one should refrain from doing it at that time. This abstention is not for the sake of the conscience of the person who is free but for the sake of another person's conscience.

Fourthly, what is done in freedom or in restriction should be done in thanksgiving and to the glory of God.

Colossians 2:16-23

> Let no man therefore judge you in meat, or in drink, or in respect of a feast day or a new moon or a sabbath day: which are a shadow of the things to come; but the body is Christ's. Let no man rob you of your prize by a voluntary humility and worshipping of the angels, dwelling in the things which he hath seen, vainly puffed up by his fleshly mind, and not holding fast the Head, from whom all the body, being supplied and knit together through the joints and bands, increaseth with the increase of God.
>
> If ye died with Christ from the rudiments of the world, why, as though living in the world, do ye subject yourselves to ordinances, Handle not, nor taste, nor touch (all which things are to perish with the using), after the precepts and doctrines of men? Which things have indeed a show of wisdom in will-worship, and humility, and severity to the body; but are not of any value against the indulgence of the flesh.

We learn first of all that the practice of liberty is the superior way of life. The need for living by a set of rules is nowhere condemned, but it is not the biblical ideal.

Secondly, since all amoral issues are clean in and of themselves, the person who has liberty is never to allow himself to submit to judgment in amoral things but is to continue in the superior way of living.

Thirdly, living by rules is a sign of immaturity. For the stronger believer to subject himself to these rudiments is to revert to a state of immaturity.

Fourthly, to subject oneself to the rules behind amoral issues is to subject oneself to human precepts and rules, not to those of the Spirit. It is to go back to living in a way that the world lives.

Fifthly, living by these rules seems to show wisdom and self-abasement, but in reality they are no help against the lusts of the flesh. One is thus not living by the Spirit but by his own efforts.

Summary

To summarize what all these passages have been saying:

a. All amoral things in themselves are clean and not sinful. There is nothing inherent in cards, dice, wine, or other things of that nature that would make them wrong for Christians to use.

b. The stronger and more mature believer is the one who is free to do all those things, feeling no pangs of conscience.

c. The weaker believer is the one who has problems with amoral things and so refrains.

d. The weaker believer is not to condemn the stronger believer for participating, nor is the stronger believer to look down upon the weaker for not being able to participate.

e. While the life of liberty is encouraged as superior, living by a set of rules is in itself never condemned, only discouraged.

f. The situation ethics for the stronger believer are based on the principle of how an action in a given situation will affect another; primarily how it will affect a fellow believer, but also how it will affect an unbeliever.

g. There can be no set rule or principle which will work in every situation other than the principle of love. But the action must depend upon the situation.

CONCLUSION

The biblical pattern and ideal for the believer is first of all obedience to the Law of Christ. By this we mean all those rules that are clearly stated and are applicable for the New Testament believer. Concerning those things which are not specifically mentioned in the Law of Christ, the amoral things, there is freedom. But since "not all men have this knowledge," those who have problems with amoral things are required to refrain from them. One believer has as much right to refrain from certain things as another believer has to do them. A person who conducts his life by a set of rules is not necessarily a legalist.

The unbiblical extent is when a person who does live by a set of rules then demands that all believers live by the same rules to prove their faith. It is at this point that he becomes a legalist and goes contrary to Scripture; for by demanding this, his conscience now becomes the judge of another's liberty:

> Conscience, I say, not thine own, but the other's; for why is my liberty judged by another conscience? (I Cor. 10:29)

By the same token, if a person who is free demands that all believers practice the same freedom, he too then becomes a legalist.

The biblical pattern then is not total abstention nor total indulgence, but moderation tempered with sensitivity to the needs of fellow believers and to the leading of the Holy Spirit. If this had been the pattern of the local church throughout the centuries, it would have had less problems for itself and for many a Hebrew Christian. It is especially in the area of legalism that the Hebrew Christian can be used in a local church to re-educate the members in the truth concerning these things, always forcing them back to the Scriptures.

Postscript: The Matter of Stumblingblocks

When biblical support is lacking, a favorite retreat used by those who wish to uphold a set of rules is to appeal to the stumblingblocks. We are not to be stumblingblocks. If we go to a movie, drink wine, or dance, we become a stumblingblock, and therefore we should not do these things at all. The fact that sometimes *not* doing these things can also be a stumblingblock is not recognized or considered. It is total abstention and that is that.

It is sin to be a stumblingblock. But I think a distinction needs to be made between a biblical stumblingblock and a stumbingblock created by the church. The stumblingblocks found in the Scripture always arise out of the culture of the people, such as eating meat sacrificed to idols. Doing something that goes against the cultural grain of the people around us is a stumblingblock, and abstinence should be practiced. Therefore I would not eat a ham sandwich in the Mea Shearim (ultra-orthodox) quarter of Jerusalem. But even here total abstention is not the answer. Eating meat sacrificed to idols was permissible in certain situations, and I have no problem eating a ham sandwich in Harlem where the culture is not against it.

Most of the things now called stumblingblocks have not risen out of the culture of the people but were church-created; these types are not valid biblical stumblingblocks. To see what a church-created stumblingblock is, we will use the example of movies.

First Step: Movies appear in human history.
Second Step: The church condemns this new thing under the sun and says Christians are not to go.
Third Step: Soon the community around the local church learns that according to the church, Christians do not go to movies.
Fourth Step: Now, if a Christian goes to movies, he becomes a stumblingblock.

This is a church-created stumblingblock and not one that arose out of the culture of the people. If the church had kept quiet, movies would never have become a stumblingblock. Thus, this is not a valid biblical stumblingblock. Instead of continuing in this type of error, it would be far nobler for the church to apologize for doing the wrong thing in condemning movies and correct the doctrinal error. The church has done this previously with eyeglasses and cars, and now it is time to do so with these other matters as well.

APPENDIX

A HEBREW CHRISTIAN
WEDDING SERVICE

THE SETTING

Only four things are required for a proper setting:

> the Hupah (canopy)
> wine bottle
> two wine goblets

The Hupah can either be held by four men with poles, or the poles can be fastened to the ground or hung from the ceiling.

Facing the Hupah, a small table should be placed to the left and on it should be placed the wine bottle and the two wine goblets within easy reach of the best man.

All other decorations for the setting are optional.

THE PROCESSIONAL

At the beginning of the processional, the minister should already be under the Hupah.

If there are attendants, they now also march in one at a time, beginning with the male and alternating between the sexes. Male attendants will line up on the bridegroom's side and female attendants on the bride's side. All attendants, except for the best man and maid of honor, are to march in with lighted candles. The latter two will carry the rings.

The bridegroom is led by his parents or by their representatives, or marches in by himself under the Hupah and faces the minister on his right.

When the bridegroom begins his march, the *minister shall say*:

Baruch Haba—May he who cometh be blessed.

When the bridegroom arrives under the Hupah, *the minister shall say*:

He who is supremely mighty;
He who is supremely praised;
He who is supremely great;
May He bless this bridegroom and bride.

The bride is led by her parents or by their representatives, or marches in by herself under the Hupah to the right of the bridegroom and facing the minister's left.

When the bride begins her march, *the minister shall say*:

Baruch Haba-ah—May she who cometh be blessed.

When the bride arrives under the Hupah, *the minister shall say*:

Mighty is our God
Auspicious signs and good fortune;
Praiseworthy is the bridegroom,
Praiseworthy and handsome is the bride.

When all are in their place, *the minister shall say*:

Friends: we are gathered in the sight of God and before these witnesses to join this man and this woman in holy matrimony; a state not to be entered into ill-advisedly or lightly, but reverently, discreetly, and in the fear of God.

Let us pray.

Jesus of Nazareth, our Messiah and the Messiah of Israel, come by thy Spirit to this marriage, we beseech thee, as to that of Cana of old. And give to those that marry a due sense of the obligations they are now about to assume. With true intent and in utter unreserve of love may they plight their troth and henceforth be helps meet for each other till death do them part. For Jesus our Messiah's sake. Amen.

An address may be delivered by the minister at this time. When the address is complete, *the minister shall say:*
Into this holy estate of matrimony these two persons come now to be joined. If any just cause can be shown why they may not be lawfully joined together, I charge that it now be made known.

THE BETROTHEL BENEDICTIONS

If there is no objections, the best man shall fill the first goblet with wine.

Then *the minister shall say:*
Praised be Thou, O Lord our God, King of the universe, Who hast created the fruit of the vine.

Praised be Thou, O Lord our God, King of the universe, Who hast sanctified us with thy commandments, and hast commanded us concerning forbidden connections and hast forbidden us those who are merely betrothed, but hast allowed to us those lawfully married to us through Hupah and betrothel. Praised are thou, O Lord, Who sanctifiest thy people Israel through Hupah and betrothel.

The best man shall now take the first goblet of wine and shall give a taste of it to the bridegroom and the bride.

The minister shall then say to the bridegroom:
_____ (name in full) _____, do you of your own free will and consent take this woman _____ (name in full) _____ to be thy wedded wife from this day forward, for better, for worse, for richer, for poorer, in sickness and in health; to live together after God's holy commandment? Wilt thou love her, comfort her, honor her, cherish her, and keep her; and forsaking all others, cleave thee only unto her, so long as ye both shall live?

The bridegroom shall say:
I do.

The minister shall now say to the bride:
_____ (name in full) _____, do you of your own free will and consent take this man _____ (name in full) _____ to be thy wedded husband, from this day forward, for better, for worse, for richer, for poorer, in sickness and in health, to live together after God's holy commandment? Wilt thou love him, honor him, inspire him, cherish him, and keep him; and forsaking all others, cleave thee only unto him, as long as ye both shall live?

The bride shall say:
I do.

The minister shall appoint two witnesses to witness the betrothel. If there are attendants, the best man and the maid of honor shall serve as the two witnesses.

The minister shall say:
The two witnesses will now approach the Hupah.

The two witnesses will step under the Hupah behind the bridegroom and the bride.

The minister shall say to the bridegroom:
You will now wed the bride in the presence of the two witnesses by placing the ring upon the fourth finger of her left hand and say to her:

Behold, with this ring you are wed to me in accordance with the laws of Israel in the name of the Father, the Son, and the Holy Spirit.

The best man will hand the ring to the bridegroom and while putting the ring on the left hand of the bride, *the bridegroom shall say:*

Behold, with this ring you are wed to me in accordance with the laws of Israel in the name of the Father, the Son, and the Holy Spirit.

The minister shall say to the bride:
You will now wed the bridegroom in the presence of the two witnesses by placing the ring upon the fourth finger of his left hand and say to him:

> Behold, with this ring you are wed to me in accordance with the laws of Israel in the name of the Father, the Son, and the Holy Spirit.

The maid of honor shall give the ring to the bride and while putting the ring on the left hand of the bridegroom, *the bride shall say*:

> Behold, with this ring you are wed to me in accordance with the laws of Israel in the name of the Father, the Son, and the Holy Spirit.

The minister shall say:
Forasmuch as you have now consented together in holy wedlock and have testified the same before God and these two witnesses (joining their hands), I hereby pronounce, by virtue of the authority vested in me, in the name of the Father, the Son, and the Holy Spirit, that you are husband and wife, so to live together until death do you part.

Now may God, through our Messiah Jesus, bless you, preserve you, and keep you. The Lord with His favor look upon you and fill you with all spiritual benediction and grace, that ye may enter into life everlasting.

Let us pray.
Eternal God, Creator and Preserver of all mankind, Giver of all spiritual grace, the Author of Everlasting life, send thy blessing upon these thy servants, this husband and this wife, that they may surely keep and perform the vows now made between them and may ever live faithfully in perfect love and peace together, according to thy laws. Through Jesus Christ our Messiah. Amen.

The best man will now fill the second goblet with wine.

The minister shall then say:

Praised be Thou, O Lord our God, King of the universe, Who hast created the fruit of the vine.

Praised be Thou, O Lord our God, King of the universe, Who hast created all things to Thy glory.

Praised be Thou, O Lord our God, King of the universe, Who hast created man.

Praised be Thou, O Lord our God, King of the universe, Who hast made man in Thine image after Thy likeness, and out of his very self, thou hast prepared unto him a perpetual fabric. Praised art Thou, O Lord, Who hast created man.

May she who is childless (Zion) be exceedingly glad and rejoice, when her children shall be reunited in her midst in joy. Praised be Thou, O Lord, Who gladdenest Zion through restoring her children.

Praised be Thou, O Lord our God, Who gladdenest the bridegroom and the bride.

Praised be Thou, O Lord our God, King of the universe, Who hast created joy and gladness, bridegroom and bride, rejoicing, song, pleasure and delight, love and brotherhood, peace, and fellowship. Soon may there be heard in the cities of Judah and in the streets of Jerusalem, the voice of joy and gladness, the voice of the bridegroom and the voice of the bride from the nuptial canopies, and of youths from their feast of song. Praised be Thou, O Lord, Who gladdenest the bridegroom and the bride.

The best man shall now give the bridegroom and the bride to taste of the second goblet of wine.

The best man shall then place the second goblet upon the floor. The bridegroom shall then shatter the second goblet with his foot.

The bridegroom shall then lift the bride's veil and kiss her in the presence of the two witnesses.

THE RECESSIONAL

The bridegroom and the bride, arm in arm, shall lead the recessional. The bridegroom and the bride shall be followed by the best man and the maid of honor. The best man and the maid of honor shall be followed by the other attendants. The attendants shall be followed by the minister.